THE POWER
OF AWARENESS

THE POWER
OF AWARENESS
Deluxe Edition

Neville Goddard

Includes a Biographical Essay and Timeline
by PEN Award-Winning Historian

Mitch Horowitz

MEDIA

MEDIA

Published 2022 by Gildan Media LLC
aka G&D Media
www.GandDmedia.com

Front cover design by David Rheinhardt of Pyrographx

Library of Congress Cataloging-in-Publication Data is available upon request

ISBN: 978-1-7225-0581-3

10   9   8   7   6   5   4   3   2   1

To Arthur and his beloved Verne whose awareness brought this book into being.

CONTENTS

II

Chariot of Fire: The Ideas of Neville Goddard
by Mitch Horowitz

Neville Goddard Timeline

About the Authors

I

THE
POWER OF
AWARENESS

This book is to reveal your infinite power, against which no earthly force is of the slightest significance. It is to show you who you are, your purpose and your destiny.

1

I AM

"All things when they are admitted are
made manifest by the light: for everything
that is made manifest is light."

EPH. 5:13

The "light" is consciousness. Consciousness is *one*, manifesting in legions of forms or levels of consciousness. There is no one that is not *all* that is, for consciousness, though expressed in an infinite series of levels is not divisional. There is no real separation or gap in consciousness. 'I AM' cannot be divided. I may conceive myself to be a rich man, a poor man, a beggar man or a thief, but the center of my being remains the same regardless of the concept I hold of myself. At the center of manifestation there is only one 'I AM' manifesting in legions of forms or concepts of itself and 'I am that I am.'

'I AM' is the self definition of the absolute, the foundation on which everything rests. 'I AM' is the first cause-substance. 'I AM' is the self definition of God.

"I AM hath sent me unto you" "I AM THAT I AM"

"Be still and know that I AM God."

'I AM' is a feeling of permanent awareness. The very center of consciousness is the feeling of 'I AM.' I may forget *who* I am, *where* I am, *what* I am, but I cannot forget that I AM. The awareness of *being* remains regardless of the degree of forgetfulness of who, where and what I am.

'I AM' is that which, amid unnumbered forms, is ever the same. This great discovery of cause reveals that, good or bad, man is actually the arbiter of his own fate, and that it is his concept of himself that determines the world in which he lives. In other words, if you are experiencing ill health, knowing the truth about cause, you cannot attribute the illness to anything other than to the particular arrangement of the basic cause-substance, an arrangement which is defined by your concept 'I am unwell.' This is why you are told "Let the weak man say, 'I am strong.'" Joel 3.10, for by his assumption, the cause-substance—'I AM'—is rearranged and must, therefore, manifest that which its rearrangement affirms. This principle governs every aspect of your life, be it social, financial, intellectual or spiritual.

'I AM' is that reality to which, whatever happens, we must turn for an explanation of the phenomena of life. It is 'I AM's' concept of itself that determines the form and scenery of its existence. Everything depends upon its attitude towards itself; that which it will not affirm as true of itself cannot awaken in its world. That is, your concept of yourself, such as 'I am strong," "I am secure," "I am loved," determines the world in which you live. In other words, when you say 'I am a man, I am a father, I am an American,' you are not defining different 'I AMs;' you are defining different concepts or arrangements of the one cause-substance—the one 'I AM.' Even in the phenomena of nature, if the tree were articulate it would say 'I am a tree, an apple tree, a fruitful tree.'

When you know that consciousness is the one and only reality—conceiving itself to be something good, bad or indifferent, and becoming that which it conceived itself to be—you are free from the tyranny of second causes, free from the belief that there are causes outside of your own mind that can affect your life.

In the state of consciousness of the individual is found the explanation of the phenomena of life. If man's concept of himself were different, everything in his world would be different. His concept of himself being what it is, everything in his world must be as it is.

Thus it is abundantly clear that there is only *one* I AM and *you* are that I AM. And while *I AM is infinite*, you, by your concept of yourself, are displaying only a limited aspect of the infinite 'I AM.'

> "Build thee more stately mansions, O my soul,
>   As the swift seasons roll!
> Leave thy low-vaulted past!
> Let each new temple, nobler than the last,
>   Shut thee from heaven with a dome more vast
>   Till thou at length art free,
> Leaving thine outgrown shell by life's unresting sea!"

2

CONSCIOUSNESS

It is only by a change of consciousness, by actually changing your concept of yourself that you can "build more stately mansions"—the manifestations of higher and higher concepts. (By manifesting is meant experiencing the results of these concepts in your world). It is of vital importance to understand clearly just what consciousness is.

The reason lies in the fact that *consciousness is the one and only reality, it is the first and only cause-substance of the phenomena of life.* Nothing has existence for man save through the consciousness he has of it. Therefore, it is to consciousness you must turn, for it is the only foundation on which the phenomena of life can be explained.

If we accept the idea of a first cause, it would follow that the evolution of that cause could never result in anything foreign to itself. That is, if the first cause-substance is light, all its evolutions, fruits and manifestations would remain light. The first cause-substance being consciousness, all its evolutions, fruits and phenomena must remain consciousness. All that could be observed would be a higher or lower form or variation of the same thing. In other words, if your consciousness is the only reality, it must also be the *only* substance. Consequently, what appears to you as circumstances, conditions and even material objects are really only the products of your own consciousness. Nature, then, as a thing or a complex of things external to your mind, must be rejected. You and your environment cannot be regarded as existing separately. You and your world are *one*.

Therefore, you must turn from the objective appearance of things to the *subjective center* of things, your consciousness, if you truly desire to know the cause of the phenomena of life, and how to use this knowledge to realize your fondest dreams. In the midst of the apparent contradictions, antagonisms and contrasts of your life, *there is only one principle at work*, only your consciousness operating. Difference does not consist in variety of substance, but in variety of arrangement of the same cause-substance, your consciousness.

The world moves with motiveless necessity. By this is meant that it has no motive of its own, but is under the necessity of manifesting your concept, the arrangement of your mind, and *your mind is always arranged in the image of all you believe and consent to as true*. The rich man, poor man, beggar man or thief are not different minds, but different arrangements of the same mind, in the same sense that a piece of steel when magnetized differs not in substance from its demagnetized state but in the arrangement and order of its molecules. A single electron revolving in a specified orbit constitutes the unit of magnetism. When a piece of steel or anything else is demagnetized, the revolving electrons have not stopped. Therefore, the magnetism has not gone out of existence. There is only a rearrangement of the particles, so that they produce no outside or perceptible effect. When particles are arranged at random, mixed up in all directions, the substance is said to be demagnetized; but when particles are marshalled in ranks so that a number of them face in one direction, the substance is a magnet. Magnetism is not generated; it is displayed. *Health, wealth, beauty and genius are not created; they are only manifested* by the arrangement of your mind—that is, by your concept of yourself. The importance of this in your daily life should be immediately apparent.

The basic nature of the primal cause is consciousness. Therefore, the ultimate substance of all things is *consciousness*.

3

POWER OF ASSUMPTION

Man's chief delusion is his conviction that there are *causes other than his own state of consciousness*. All that befalls a man—all that is done by him, all that comes from him—happens as a result of his state of consciousness. A man's consciousness is all that he thinks and desires and loves, all that he believes is true and consents to. That is why a change of consciousness is necessary before you can change your outer world. Rain falls as a result of a change in the temperature in the higher regions of the atmosphere, so, in like manner, a change of circumstance happens as a result of a change in your state of consciousness.

"Be ye transformed by the renewing of your mind."

To be transformed, the whole basis of your thoughts must change. But your thoughts cannot change unless you have *new ideas*, for you think from your ideas. All transformation begins with an intense, burning desire to be transformed. The first step in the 'renewing of the mind' is *desire*. You must want to be different before you can begin to change yourself. Then you must *make your future dream a present fact.* You do this by *assuming the feeling of your wish fulfilled.* By desiring to be other than what you are, you can create an ideal of the person you want to be and *assume that you are already that person.* If this assumption is persisted in until it becomes your dominant feeling, the attainment of your ideal is inevitable. The ideal you hope to achieve is always ready for an incarnation, but unless you yourself offer it human parentage it is incapable of birth. Therefore, your attitude should be one in which—having desired to express a higher state—you alone accept the task of incarnating this new and greater value of yourself.

In giving birth to your ideal you must bear in mind that the methods of mental and spiritual knowledge are entirely different. This is a point that is truly understood by probably not more than one person in a million. You know a thing mentally by looking at it from the outside, by comparing it with other things, by analyzing it and defining it; whereas you can know a thing spiritually only by becoming it. You must be the thing itself and not merely talk about it or look at it. You must be like the moth in search of his idol, the flame,

> "who spurred with true desire, plunging at once into the
> sacred fire, folded his wings within, till he became one
> colour and one substance with the flame. He only knew
> the flame who in it burned, and only he could tell who
> ne'er to tell returned."

Just as the moth in his desire to know the flame was willing to destroy himself, so must you in becoming a new person be willing to die to your present self.

You must be conscious of *being* healthy if you are to know what health is. You must be conscious of *being* secure if you are to know what security is. Therefore, to incarnate a new and greater value of yourself, you must assume that you already are what you want to be and then live by faith in this assumption—which is not yet incarnate in the body of your life—in confidence that this new value or state of consciousness will become incarnated through your absolute fidelity to the assumption that you are that which you desire to be. This is what wholeness means, what integrity means. They mean submission of the whole self to the feeling of the wish fulfilled in certainty that that new state of consciousness is the renewing of mind which transforms. There is no order in Nature corresponding to this willing submission of the self to the ideal beyond the self. Therefore, it is the height of folly to expect the incarnation of a new and greater concept of self to come about by natural evolutionary process. That which requires a state of consciousness to produce its effect obviously cannot be effected without such a state of consciousness, and in your ability to assume the feeling of a greater life, to assume a new concept of yourself, *you possess what the rest of Nature does not possess—Imagination— the instrument by which you create your world.* Your imagination is the instrument, the means, whereby your redemption from slavery, sickness and poverty is effected. If you refuse to assume the responsibility of the incarnation of a new and higher concept of yourself, then you *reject the means, the only means, whereby your redemption—that is, the attainment of your ideal—can be effected.*

Imagination is the only redemptive power in the universe. However, your nature is such that it is optional to you whether you remain in your present concept of yourself (a hungry being longing for freedom, health and security) or choose to become the instrument of your own redemption, imagining yourself as that which you want to be, and thereby satisfying your hunger and redeeming yourself.

> *"O be strong then, and brave, pure, patient and true;*
> *The work that is yours let no other hand do.*
> *For the strength for all need is faithfully given*
> *From the fountain within you—the Kingdom*
> *of Heaven."*

4

DESIRE

The changes which take place in your life *as a result of your changed concept of yourself* always appear to the unenlightened to be the result, not of a change of your consciousness, but of chance, outer cause or coincidence. However, the only fate governing your life is the fate determined by your own concepts, your own assumptions; for an assumption, *though false*, if persisted in will harden into fact. The ideal you seek and hope to attain will not manifest itself, will not be realized by you, until you have imagined that you are already that ideal. There is no escape for you except by a radical psychological transformation of yourself, except by your assumption of the feeling of your wish fulfilled. Therefore, make results or accomplishments the crucial test of your ability to use your imagination.

Everything depends on your attitude towards yourself. *That which you will not affirm as true of yourself can never be realized by you* for that attitude alone is the necessary condition by which you realize your goal.

All transformation is based upon suggestion and this can work only where you lay yourself completely open to an influence. You must abandon yourself to your ideal as a woman abandons herself to love, for complete abandonment of self to it is the way to union with your ideal. You must assume the feeling of the wish fulfilled until your assumption has all the sensory vividness of reality. *You must imagine that you are already experiencing what you desire.* That is, you must assume the feeling of the fulfillment of your desire until you are possessed by it and this feeling crowds all other ideas out of your consciousness.

The man who is not prepared for the conscious plunge into the assumption of the wish fulfilled in the faith that it is the only way to the realization of his dream is not yet ready to live *consciously* by the law of assumption, although there is no doubt that he does live by the law of assumption unconsciously. But for you who accept this principle and are ready to live by consciously assuming that your wish is already fulfilled, the adventure of life begins. To reach a higher level of being, you must assume a higher concept of yourself.

If you will not imagine yourself as other than what you are, then you remain as you are,

> *"for if ye believe not that I am He, ye shall die in your sins."*

If you do not believe that you are He (the person you want to be) then you remain as you are. Through the faithful systematic cultivation of the feeling of the wish fulfilled, *desire becomes the promise of its own fulfillment.* The assumption of the feeling of the wish fulfilled makes the future dream a present fact.

5

THE TRUTH THAT SETS YOU FREE

The drama of life is a psychological one in which all the conditions, circumstances and events of your life are brought to pass by your assumptions.

Since your life is determined by your assumptions you are forced to recognize the fact that you are either a slave to your assumptions or their master. To become the master of your assumptions is the key to undreamed of freedom and happiness. You can attain this mastery by deliberate conscious control of your imagination. You determine your assumptions in this way: Form a mental image, a picture of the state desired, of the person you want to be. Concentrate your attention upon the feeling that you are already that person. First, visualize the picture in your consciousness. Then *feel* yourself to be in that state as though it actually formed your surrounding world. By your imagination that which was a mere mental image is changed into a seemingly solid reality.

The great secret is a controlled imagination and a well sustained attention firmly and repeatedly focused on the object to be accomplished. It cannot be emphasized too much that, by creating an ideal within your mental sphere, by assuming that you are already that ideal, *you identify yourself with it and thereby transform yourself into its image.* This was called by the ancient teachers, "Subjection to the will of God" or "Resting in the Lord", and the only true test of "Resting in the Lord" is that all who *do* rest are inevitably transformed into the image of that in which they rest. You become according to your resigned will, and your resigned will is your concept of yourself and all that you consent to and accept as true. You, assuming the feeling of your wish fulfilled and continuing therein, take upon yourself the results of that state; not assuming the feeling of your wish fulfilled, you are ever free of the results.

When you understand the redemptive function of imagination, *you hold in your hands the key to the solution of all your problems.* Every phase of your life is made by the exercise of your imagination. Determined imagination alone is the means of your progress, of the fulfilling of your dreams. *It is the beginning and end of all creating. The great secret is a controlled imagination and a well sustained attention firmly and repeatedly focused on the feeling of the wish fulfilled until it fills the mind and crowds all other ideas out of consciousness.* What greater gifts could be given you than to be told the Truth that will set you free. *The Truth that sets you free is that you can experience in imagination what you desire to experience in reality, and by maintaining this experience in imagination your desire will become an actuality.*

You are limited only by your uncontrolled imagination and lack of attention to the feeling of your wish fulfilled. When the imagination is not controlled and the attention not steadied on the feeling of the wish fulfilled, then no amount of prayer or piety or invocation will produce the desired effect. When you can call up at will whatsoever image you please, when the forms of your imagination are as vivid to you as the forms of nature, you are master of your fate.

> *Visions of beauty and splendor,*
> *Forms of a long-lost race,*
> *Sounds and faces and voices,*
> *From the fourth dimension of space—*
> *And on through the universe boundless,*
> *Our thoughts go lightning shod—*
> *Some call it imagination,*
> *And others call it God.*

6

ATTENTION

"A double minded man is unstable in all his ways."

JAMES 1:8

Attention is forceful in proportion to the narrowness of its focus, that is, when it is obsessed with a single idea or sensation. It is steadied and powerfully focused only by such an adjustment of the mind as permits you to see one thing only, for you steady the attention and increase its power by confining it. *The desire which realizes itself is always a desire upon which attention is exclusively concentrated,* for an idea is endowed with power only in proportion to the degree of attention fixed on it. Concentrated observation is the attentive attitude directed towards some specific end. The attentive attitude involves selection, for when you pay attention it signifies that you have decided to focus your attention on one object or state rather than on another.

Therefore, when you know what you want you must deliberately focus your attention on the feeling of your wish fulfilled until that feeling fills the mind and crowds all other ideas out of consciousness.

The power of attention is the measure of your inner force. Concentrated observation of one thing shuts out other things and causes them to disappear. *The great secret of success is to focus the attention on the feeling of the wish fulfilled without permitting any distraction.* All progress depends upon an *increase* of attention. The ideas which impel you to action are those which dominate the consciousness, those which possess the attention.

> *"This one thing I do, forgetting those things
> that are behind, I press toward the mark."*

This means you, this one thing you can do, "forgetting those things that are behind." You can press toward the mark of filling your mind with the feeling of the wish fulfilled.

To the unenlightened man this will seem to be all fantasy, yet *all progress comes from those who do not take the accepted view, nor accept the world as it is.* As was stated heretofore, if you can imagine what you please, and if the forms of your thought are as vivid as the forms of nature, you are by virtue of the power of your imagination, master of your fate.

Your imagination is you yourself and the world as your imagination sees it is the real world.

When you set out to master the movements of attention, which must be done if you would successfully alter the course of observed events, it is then you realize how little control you exercise over your imagination and how much it is dominated by sensory impressions and by a drifting on the tides of idle moods.

To aid in mastering the control of your attention practice this exercise. Night after night, just before you drift off to sleep, strive to hold your attention on the activities of the day *in reverse order*. Focus your attention on the last thing you did, that is, getting *in* to bed and then move it backward in time over the events until you reach the first event of the day, getting *out* of bed. This is no easy exercise, but just as specific exercises greatly help in developing specific muscles, this will greatly help in developing the "muscle" of your attention. Your attention must be developed, controlled and concentrated in order to change your concept of yourself successfully and thereby change your future. Imagination is able to do anything *but only according to the internal direction of your attention*. If you persist night after night, sooner or later you will awaken in yourself a centre of power and become conscious of your greater self, the real you. Attention is developed by repeated exercise or habit. Through habit an action becomes easier, and so in course of time gives rise to a facility or faculty, which can then be put to higher uses.

When you attain control of the internal direction of your attention, you will no longer stand in shallow water but will launch out into the deep of life. You will walk in the assumption of the wish fulfilled as on a foundation more solid even than earth.

7

ATTITUDE

Experiments recently conducted by Merle Lawrence (Princeton) and Adelbert Ames (Dartmouth) in the latter's psychology laboratory at Hanover, N. H., prove that what you see when you look at something *depends not so much on what is there as on the assumption you make when you look*. Since what we believe to be the "real" physical world is actually only an "assumptive" world, it is not surprising that these experiments prove that what appears to be solid reality is actually the result of "expectations" or "assumptions." Your assumptions determine not only what you see but also what you do, for they govern all your conscious and subconscious movements towards the fulfillment of themselves. Over a century ago this truth was stated by Emerson as follows:

> *"As the world was plastic and fluid in the hands of God, so it is ever to so much of his attributes as we bring to it. To ignorance and sin, it is flint. They adapt themselves to it as they may, but in proportion as a man has anything in him divine, the firmament flows before him and takes his signet and form."*

Your assumption is the hand of God moulding the firmament into the image of that which you assume. The assumption of the wish fulfilled is the high tide which lifts you easily off the bar of the senses where you have so long lain stranded. It lifts the mind into prophecy in the full right sense of the word; and if you have that controlled imagination and absorbed attention which it is possible to attain, you may be sure that all your assumption implies will come to pass.

When William Blake wrote,

> *"What seems to be, is, to those to whom it seems to be"*

he was only repeating the eternal truth,

> *"there is nothing unclean of itself: but to him that*
> *esteemeth anything to be unclean, to him it is unclean."*
>
> ROM. 14:14

Because there is nothing unclean *of itself* (or clean of itself) you should assume the best and think only of that which is lovely and of good report. It is not superior insight but ignorance of this law of assumption if you read into the greatness of men some littleness with which you may be familiar—or into some situation or circumstance an unfavorable conviction. *Your particular relationship to another influences your assumption with respect to that other and makes you see in him that which you do see. If you can change your opinion of another, then what you now believe of him cannot be* absolutely true but is only *relatively* true. The following is an actual case history illustrating how the law of assumption works:

One day a costume designer described to me her difficulties in working with a prominent theatrical producer. She was convinced that he unjustly criticized and rejected her best work and that often he was deliberately rude and unfair to her. Upon hearing her story, I explained that if she found the other rude and unfair, it was a sure sign that she, herself, was wanting and that it was not the producer, but herself that was in need of a new attitude. I told her that the power of this law of assumption and its practical application could be discovered only through experience and that only by assuming that the situation was *already* what she wanted it to be could she prove that she could bring about the change desired. Her employer was merely bearing witness, telling her by his behavior what her *concept* of him was. I suggested that it was quite probable that she was carrying on conversations with him *in her mind* which were filled with criticism and recriminations. There was no doubt but that she was mentally arguing with the producer, for others only echo that which we whisper to them in secret. I asked her if it was not true that she talked to him *mentally* and if so what those conversations were like. She confessed that every morning on her way to the theatre she told him just what she thought of him in a way she would never have dared address him in person. The intensity and force of her mental arguments with him automatically established his behavior towards her. She began to realize that all of us carry on mental conversations, but, unfortunately on most occasions these conversations are argumentative . . . that we have only to observe the passerby on the street to prove this assertion . . . that so many people are mentally engrossed in conversation and few appear to be happy about it, but the very intensity of their feeling must lead them quickly to the unpleasant incident they, themselves, have mentally created and therefore must now encounter. When she realized what she had been doing, she agreed to change her attitude and to live this law faithfully by assuming that her job was highly satisfactory and her relationship with the producer was a very happy one. To do this she agreed that before going to sleep at night, on her way to work, and at other intervals during the day she would *imagine* that he had congratulated her on her fine designs and that she, in turn, had thanked him for his praise and kindness. To her great delight she soon discovered for herself that her own attitude was the cause of all that befell her.

The behavior of her employer miraculously reversed itself. His attitude, echoing, as it had always done, that which she had assumed, now reflected her *changed* concept of him.

What she did was by the power of her imagination. Her persistent assumption influenced his behavior and determined his attitude toward her. With the passport of desire and on the wings of a controlled imagination she traveled into the future of her own predetermined experience.

Thus we see it is not facts, but that which we create in our imagination which shapes our lives, for most of the conflicts of the day are due to the want of a little imagination to cast the beam out of our own eye. It is the exact and literal minded who live in a fictitious world. As this designer, by her controlled imagination, started the subtle change in her employer's mind, so can we, by the control of our imagination and wisely directed feeling solve our problems.

By the intensity of her imagination and feeling the designer cast a kind of enchantment on her producer's mind and caused him to think that his generous praise originated with him. Often our most elaborate and original thoughts are determined by another.

> *"We should never be certain that it was not some woman treading in the wine-press who began that subtle change in men's mind, or that the passion did not begin in the mind of some shepherd boy, lighting up his eyes for a moment before it ran upon its way."*
>
> WILLIAM BUTLER YEATS

8

RENUNCIATION

*"There is no coal of character so dead that it will
not glow and flame if but slightly turned."*

"Resist not evil."

*"Whosoever shall smite thee on thy right
cheek, turn to him the other also."*

There is a great difference between *resisting evil and renouncing it.*

When you resist evil, you give it your attention, you continue to make it real. When you renounce evil you take your attention from it and give your attention to what you want. Now is the time to control your imagination and

> *"Give beauty for ashes, joy for mourning, praise for the
> spirit of heaviness, that they might be called trees of
> righteousness, the planting of the Lord that He might
> be glorified."*

You give beauty for ashes when you concentrate your attention on things as you would like them to be rather than on things as they are. You give joy for mourning when you maintain a joyous attitude regardless of unfavorable circumstances. You give praise for the spirit of heaviness when you maintain a confident attitude instead of succumbing to despondency. In this quotation the Bible uses the word tree as a synonym for man. You become a tree of righteousness when the above mental states are a permanent part of your consciousness. You are a planting of the Lord when all your thoughts are *true* thoughts. He is "I AM" as described in Chapter One. "I AM" is glorified when your highest concept of yourself is manifested.

When you have discovered your own controlled imagination to be your saviour, your attitude will be completely altered without any diminution of religious feeling and you will say of your controlled imagination

> *"Behold this vine. I found it a wild tree, whose wanton*
> *strength had swollen into irregular twigs. But I pruned*
> *the plant and it grew temperate in its vain expense of*
> *useless leaves, and knotted as you see into these clean*
> *full clusters to repay the hand that wisely wounded it."*

By vine is meant your imagination which in its uncontrolled state, expends its energy in useless or destructive thoughts and feelings. But you, just as the vine is pruned by cutting away its useless branches and roots, prune your imagination *by withdrawing your attention from all unlovely and destructive ideas and concentrating on the ideal you wish to attain.* The happier more noble life you will experience will be the result of wisely pruning your own imagination. Yes, be pruned of all unlovely thoughts and feelings that you may:

> *"Think truly, and thy thoughts shall the world's famine feed; Speak truly, and each word of thine shall be a fruitful seed; Live truly, and thy life shall be a great and noble creed."*

9

PREPARING
YOUR PLACE

"And all mine are thine, and thine are mine;"

JOHN 17:10

"Thrust in thy sickle, and reap; for the time is come
for thee to reap; for the harvest of the earth is ripe."

REV. 14:15

All is yours. Do not go seeking for that which you are. Appropriate it, claim it, assume it. *Everything* depends upon your concept of yourself. That which you do not claim as true of yourself, cannot be realized by you. The promise is

"Whosoever hath, to him it shall be given, and he shall
have more abundance; but whosoever hath not, from
him shall be taken away even that which he seemeth to
have."

Hold fast, in your imagination, to all that is lovely and of good report for the lovely and the good are essential in your life if it is to be worthwhile. Assume it. You do this by imagining that you *already are* what you want to be—and *already have* what you want to have.

"*As a man thinketh in his heart so is he.*"

Be still and know that you are that which you desire to be, and you will never have to search for it.

In spite of your appearance of freedom of action, you obey, as everything else does, the law of assumption. Whatever you may think of the question of free will, the truth is *your experiences throughout your life are determined by your assumptions*—whether conscious or unconscious. An assumption *builds a bridge of incidents that lead inevitably to the fulfillment of itself.*

Man believes the future to be the natural development of the past. But the law of assumption clearly shows that this is not the case. Your assumption places you psychologically where you are not *physically*; then your senses pull you back from where you were psychologically to where you are physically. *It is these psychological forward motions that produce your physical forward motions in time.* Pre-cognition permeates all the scriptures of the world.

> "*In my Father's house are many mansions; If it were not so, I would have told you. I go to prepare a place for you. And if I go and prepare a place for you, I will come again and receive you unto myself: that where I am,*

there ye may be also And now I have told you before
it came to pass, that, when it is come to pass ye might
believe."

JOHN 14:2, 3, 29

The "I" in this quotation is your imagination which goes into the future, into one of the many mansions. Mansion is the state desired . . . telling of an event before it occurs *physically* is simply feeling yourself into the state desired until it has the tone of reality. *You go and prepare a place for yourself by imagining yourself into the feeling of your wish fulfilled.* Then, you speed from this state of the wish fulfilled—where you have not been physically—back to where you were physically a moment ago. Then, with an irresistible forward movement, you move forward across a series of events to the physical realization of your wish that where you have been in imagination, there you will be in the flesh also.

"Unto the place from whence the rivers come, thither
they return again."

ECCLES. 1:7

10

CREATION

"I am God, declaring the end from the beginning,
and from ancient times things that are not yet done."

ISAIAH 46:10

Creation is finished. Creativeness is only a deeper receptiveness, for the entire contents of all time and all space while experienced in a time sequence actually co-exist in an infinite and eternal now. In other words, all that you ever have been or ever will be—in fact, all that mankind ever was or ever will be, exists *now*. This is what is meant by creation and the statement that creation is finished means that nothing is ever to be created, it is only to be manifested. *What is called creativeness is only becoming aware of what already is.* You simply become aware of increasing portions of that which already exists. The fact that you can never be anything that you are not already or experience anything not already existing explains the experience of having an acute feeling of having heard *before* what is being said, or having met *before* the person being met for the first time, or having seen *before*, a place or thing being seen for the first time.

The whole of creation exists in you and it is your destiny to become increasingly aware of its infinite wonders and to experience ever greater and grander portions of it.

If creation is finished, and all events are taking place now, the question that springs naturally to the mind is "what determines your time track?" That is, what determines the events which you encounter? And the answer is *your concept of yourself.* Concepts determine the route that attention follows.

Here is a good test to prove this fact. Assume the feeling of your wish fulfilled and observe the route that your attention follows. You will observe that as long as you remain faithful to your assumption, so long will your attention be confronted with images clearly related to that assumption. For example; if you assume that you have a wonderful business, you will notice how *in your imagination* your attention is focused on incident after incident relating to that assumption. Friends congratulate you, tell you how lucky you are. Others are envious and critical. From there your attention goes to larger offices, bigger bank balances and many other similarly related events. Persistence in this assumption will result in *actually experiencing in fact that which you assumed.*

The same is true regarding any concept. If your concept of yourself is that you are a failure you would encounter in your imagination a whole series of incidents in conformance to that concept.

Thus it is clearly seen how you, by your concept of yourself, determine your present, that is, the particular portion of creation which you now experience, and your future, that is, the particular portion of creation which you will experience.

11

INTERFERENCE

You are free to choose the concept you will accept of yourself. Therefore, you possess the power of *intervention*, the power which enables you to *alter the course of your future*. The process of rising from your present concept to a higher concept of yourself is the means of all true progress. The higher concept is waiting for you to incarnate it in the world of experience.

> *"Now unto Him that is able to do exceeding abundantly above all that we ask or think, according to the power that worketh in us. Unto him be glory."*
>
> EPH. 3:20

Him, that is able to do more than you can ask or think, is *your imagination*, and the *power that worketh in us* is *your attention*. Understanding imagination to be HIM that is able to do all that you ask and attention to be the power by which you create your world, you can now build your ideal world. Imagine yourself to be the ideal you dream of and desire. Remain attentive to this imagined state and as fast as you completely feel that you are already this ideal it will manifest itself as *reality* in your world.

"He was in the world, and the world was made by him and the world knew him not."

"The mystery hid from the ages; Christ in you, the hope of glory."

The "He", in the first of these quotations, is your imagination. As previously explained, there is only one substance. This substance is consciousness. It is your imagination which forms this substance into concepts, which concepts are then manifested as conditions, circumstances and physical objects. *Thus imagination made your world.* This supreme truth with but few exceptions, man is not conscious of.

The mystery, *Christ in you*, referred to in the second quotation, is your imagination, by which your world is molded. The hope of glory is your awareness of the ability to rise perpetually to higher levels.

Christ is not to be found in history nor in external forms. You find Christ only when you become aware of the fact that *your imagination* is the only redemptive power. When this is discovered, the "towers of dogma will have heard the trumpets of Truth, and, like the walls of Jericho, crumble to dust."

12

SUBJECTIVE
CONTROL

Your imagination is able to do all that you ask *in proportion to the degree of your attention*. All progress, all fulfillment of desire, depend upon the control and concentration of your attention. Attention may be either attracted from without or directed from within. Attention is attracted from without when you are consciously occupied with the external impressions of the immediate present. The very lines of this page are attracting your attention from without. Your attention is directed from within when you deliberately choose what you will be preoccupied with mentally. It is obvious that in the objective world your attention is not only attracted by but is constantly *directed* to external impressions. But, your control in the *subjective state* is almost non-existent, for in this state attention is usually the servant and not the master—the passenger and not the navigator—of your world. There is an enormous difference between attention directed objectively and attention directed subjectively, and the *capacity to change your future depends on the latter*. When you are able to control the movements of your attention in the subjective world you can modify or alter your life as you please. But this control cannot be achieved if you allow your attention to be attracted constantly from without. Each day, set yourself the task of deliberately withdrawing your attention from the objective world and of focusing it *subjectively*. In other words, concentrate on those thoughts or moods which you deliberately determine. Then those things that now restrict you will fade and drop away. The day you achieve control of the movements of your attention in the subjective world, you are master of your fate.

You will no longer accept the dominance of outside conditions or circumstances. You will not accept life on the basis of the world without. Having achieved control of the movements of your attention, and having discovered the mystery hid from the ages, that *Christ in you is your imagination,* you will assert the supremacy of *imagination* and put all things in subjection to it.

13

ACCEPTANCE

*"Man's Perceptions are not bounded by organs
of Perception: he perceives more than sense
(though ever so acute) can discover."*

However much you seem to be living in a material world, *you
are actually living in a world of imagination.* The outer, physical
events of life are the fruit of forgotten blossom-times—results of
previous and usually forgotten states of consciousness. They are
the ends running true to oftimes forgotten imaginative origins.

Whenever you become completely absorbed in an emotional
state you are at that moment assuming the feeling of the state
fulfilled. If persisted in, whatsoever you are intensely emotional
about you will experience in your world. These periods of absorption, of concentrated attention, are the beginnings of the things
you harvest. It is in such moments that you are exercising your
creative power—the only creative power there is. At the end of
these periods, or moments of absorption, you speed from these
imaginative states (where you have *not been* physically) to where
you were physically an instant ago. In these periods the imagined
state is so real that when you return to the objective world and find

that it is not the same as the imagined state, it is an actual shock. You have seen something in imagination with such vividness that you now wonder whether the evidence of your senses can now be believed and like Keats you ask,

> *"was it a vision or a waking dream?*
> *Fled is that music . . . Do I wake or sleep?"*

This shock reverses your time sense. By this is meant that *instead of your experience resulting from your past, it now becomes the result of being in imagination where you have not yet been physically.* In effect, this moves you across a bridge of incident to the physical realization of your imagined state. The man who at will can assume whatever state he pleases has found the keys to the Kingdom of Heaven. The keys are *desire, imagination and a steadily focused attention on the feeling of the wish fulfilled.* To such a man any undesirable objective fact is no longer a reality and the ardent wish no longer a dream.

> *"Prove me now herewith, saith the Lord of hosts, if I*
> *will not open you the windows of heaven, and pour you*
> *out a blessing, that there shall not be room enough to*
> *receive it."*
>
> MALACHI 3:10

The windows of heaven may not be opened and the treasures seized by a strong will, but they open of themselves and present their treasures as a free gift—a gift that comes when absorption reaches such a degree that it results in a feeling of complete acceptance. The passage from your present state to the feeling of your wish fulfilled is not across a gap. There is continuity between the so-called real and unreal. To cross from one state to the other, you simply extend your feelers, trust your touch and enter fully into the spirit of what you are doing.

> "Not by might nor by power but by my spirit, saith the Lord of hosts."

Assume the spirit, the feeling of the wish fulfilled, and you will have opened the windows to receive the blessing. To assume a state is to get into the spirit of it. Your triumphs will be a surprise only to those who did not know your hidden passage from the state of longing to the assumption of the wish fulfilled.

The Lord of hosts will not respond to your wish until you have assumed the feeling of already being what you want to be, for *acceptance is the channel of His action*. Acceptance is the Lord of hosts in action.

14

THE EFFORTLESS WAY

The principal of 'Least Action' governs everything in physics from the path of a planet to the path of a pulse of light. Least Action is the minimum of energy, multiplied by the minimum of time. Therefore, in moving from your present state to the state desired, you must use the minimum of energy and take the shortest possible time. Your journey from one state of consciousness to another, is a psychological one, so, to make the journey you must employ the psychological equivalent of 'Least Action' and the psychological equivalent is mere assumption.

The day you fully realize the power of assumption, you discover that it works in complete conformity with this principle. It works by means of attention, minus effort. Thus, with least action through an assumption you hurry without haste and reach your goal without effort.

Because creation is finished, *what you desire already exists*. It is excluded from view because you can see only the contents of your own consciousness. It is the function of an assumption to call back the excluded view and restore full vision. *It is not the world but your assumptions that change.* An assumption brings the invisible into sight. It is nothing more nor less than seeing with the eye of God, i.e., imagination.

"For the Lord seeth not as a man seeth, for man looketh
on the outward appearance, but the Lord looketh on
the heart."

The heart is the primary organ of sense, hence the first cause of experience. When you look "on the heart" you are looking at your assumptions: assumptions determine your experience. Watch your assumption with all diligence for out of it are the issues of life. Assumptions have the power of objective realization. Every event in the visible world is the result of an assumption or idea in the unseen world.

The present moment is all important, for it is only in the present moment that our assumptions can be controlled. The future must become the present in your mind if you would wisely operate the law of assumption. The future becomes the present when you imagine that you already are what you will be when your assumption is fulfilled. Be still (least action) and know that you are that which you desire to be. The end of longing should be Being. Translate your dream into Being. Perpetual construction of future states without the consciousness of already being them, that is, picturing your desire without actually assuming the feeling of the wish fulfilled, is the fallacy and mirage of mankind.

It is simply futile day-dreaming.

15

THE CROWN OF
THE MYSTERIES

The assumption of the wish fulfilled is the ship that carries you over the unknown seas to the fulfillment of your dream. *The assumption is everything; realization is subconscious and effortless.*

> *"Assume a virtue if you have it not."*

Act on the assumption that you already possess that which you sought.

> *"blessed is she that believed; for there shall be a performance of those things which were told her from the Lord."*

As the Immaculate Conception is the foundation of the Christian mysteries, so the Assumption is their crown. Psychologically the Immaculate Conception means the *birth of an idea* in your own consciousness unaided by another. For instance, when you have a specific wish or hunger or longing it is an immaculate conception in the sense that no physical person or thing plants it in your mind. It is self-conceived. Every man is the Mary of the Immaculate Conception and birth to his idea must give. The Assumption is the crown of the mysteries because it is the highest use of consciousness. When in imagination you assume the feeling of the wish fulfilled, *you are mentally lifted up to a higher level.* When, through your persistence, this assumption becomes actual fact, you automatically find yourself on a higher level (that is, you have achieved your desire) in your objective world. Your assumption guides all your conscious and subconscious movements towards its suggested end so inevitably that it *actually dictates the events.*

The drama of life is a psychological one and the whole of it is written and produced by *your assumptions.*

Learn the art of assumption for only in this way can you create your own happiness.

16

PERSONAL IMPOTENCE

Self-surrender is essential and by that is meant the confession of personal impotence.

"I can of mine own self do nothing."

Since creation is finished it is impossible to *force* anything into being. The example of magnetism previously given is a good illustration. You cannot make magnetism, it can only be displayed. You cannot make the *law* of magnetism. If you want to build a magnet you can do so only by conforming to the law of magnetism. In other words, you surrender yourself or yield to the law. In like manner when you use the faculty of assumption you are *conforming* to a law just as real as the law governing magnetism. *You can neither create nor change the law of assumption.* It is in this respect that you are impotent. You can only yield or conform, and since all of your experiences are the result of your assumptions, (consciously or unconsciously) the value of consciously using the power of assumption surely must be obvious.

Willingly identify yourself with that which you most desire, knowing that it will find expression through you. Yield to the feeling of the wish fulfilled and be consumed as its victim, then rise as the prophet of *the law of assumption.*

17

ALL THINGS ARE POSIBLE

It is of great significance that the truth of the principles outlined in this book have been proven time and again by the personal experiences of the Author. Throughout the past twenty-five years he has applied these principles and proved them successful in innumerable instances. He attributes to an unwavering assumption of his wish already being fulfilled every success that he has achieved. He was confident that by these fixed assumptions his desires were predestined to be fulfilled. Time and again he assumed the feeling of his wish fulfilled and continued in his assumption until that which he desired was completely realized.

Live your life in a sublime spirit of confidence and determination; disregard appearances, conditions, in fact all evidence of your senses that deny the fulfillment of your desire. Rest in the assumption that you are already what you want to be, for in that determined assumption you and your Infinite Being are merged in creative unity, *and with your Infinite Being (God) all things are possible.* God never fails.

> *"For who can stay His hand or say unto Him,*
> *'what doest thou'?"*

Through the mastery of your assumptions you are in very truth enabled to *master life*. It is thus that the ladder of life is ascended: thus the ideal is realized. The clue to the real purpose of life is to surrender yourself to your ideal with such awareness of its *reality* that you begin to live the life of the ideal and no longer your own life as it was prior to this surrender.

> *"He calleth things that are not seen as though they*
> *were, and the unseen becomes seen."*

Each assumption has its corresponding world. If you are truly observant you will notice the power of your assumptions to change circumstances which appear wholly immutable.

You, by your conscious assumptions determine the nature of the world in which you live. Ignore the present state and assume the wish fulfilled. Claim it; *it will respond*. The law of assumption is the means by which the fulfillment of your desires may be realized. Every moment of your life, *consciously or unconsciously*, you are assuming a feeling. You can no more avoid assuming a feeling than you can avoid eating and drinking. All you can do is control the nature of your assumptions.

Thus it is clearly seen that the control of your assumption is the key you now hold to an ever expanding, happier, more noble life.

18

BE YE DOERS

"Be ye doers of the word and not hearers only, deceiving your own selves. For if any be a hearer of the word, and not a doer, he is like unto a man beholding his natural face in a glass and goeth his way, and straightway forgetteth what manner of man he was. But whoso looketh into the perfect law of liberty, and continue therein, he being not a forgetful hearer but a doer of the work, this man shall be blessed in his deed."

JAMES 1:22-25

The word in this quotation means idea, concept or desire. You deceive yourself by "hearing only" when you expect your desire to be fulfilled through mere wishful thinking. Your desire is what you want to be and looking at yourself "in a glass" is *seeing yourself in imagination as that person.* Forgetting "what manner of man" you are is *failing to persist in your assumption.* The "perfect law of liberty" is the law which makes possible liberation from limitation, that is, the law of assumption. To continue in the perfect law of liberty is to persist in the assumption that your desire is already fulfilled. You are not a "forgetful hearer" when you keep the feeling of your wish fulfilled constantly alive in your consciousness. This makes you a "doer of the work" and you are blessed in your deed by the inevitable realization of your desire.

You must be *doers* of the law of assumption, for without application the most profound understanding will not produce any desired result.

Frequent reiteration and repetition of important basic truths runs through these pages. Where the law of assumption is concerned—the law that sets man free—this is a good thing. It should be made clear again and again even at the risk of repetition. The real truth seeker will welcome this aid in concentrating his attention upon the *law which sets him free*.

The parable of the Master's condemnation of the servant who neglected to use the talent given him is clear and unmistakable. Having discovered within yourself the key to the Treasure House, you should be like the good servant who by wise use multiplied by many times the talents entrusted to him. *The talent entrusted to you is the power to consciously determine your assumption.* The talent not used, like the limb not exercised, withers and finally atrophies.

What you must strive after is *being*. In order to do, it is necessary to be. *The end of yearning is to be.* Your concept of yourself can only be driven out of consciousness by *another* concept of yourself. By creating an ideal in your mind, you can identify yourself with it until you become one and the same with the ideal, thereby transforming yourself into it.

The dynamic prevails over the static; the active over the passive. One who is a doer is magnetic and therefore infinitely more creative than any who merely hear. Be among the doers.

19

ESSENTIALS

The essential points in the successful use of the law of assumption are these: First, and above all, *yearning, longing, intense burning desire.*

With all your heart you must want to be different from what you are. Intense, burning desire *is* the mainspring of action, the beginning of all successful ventures. In every great passion desire is concentrated.

> *"As the heart panteth after the water brooks, so panteth my soul after Thee, O God."*
>
> *"Blessed are they that hunger and thirst after righteousness for they shall be filled."*

Here the soul is interpreted as the sum total of all you believe, think, feel and accept as true; in other words, your present level of awareness. God means I AM, the source and fulfillment of all desire. This quotation describes how your present level of awareness longs to transcend itself. *Righteousness is the consciousness of already being what you want to be.*

Second, *cultivate physical immobility*, a physical incapacity not unlike the state described by Keats in his 'Ode to a Nightingale'.

> *"A drowsy numbness pains my senses, as though of hemlock I had drunk."*

It is a state akin to sleep, but one in which you are still in control of the direction of attention. You must learn to induce this state at will, but experience has taught that it is more easily induced after a substantial meal, or when you wake in the morning feeling very loath to arise. Then you are naturally disposed to enter this state. The value of physical immobility shows itself in the accumulation of mental force which absolute stillness brings with it. It increases your power of concentration.

> *"Be still and know that I am God."*

In fact, the greater energies of the mind seldom break forth save when the body is stilled and the door of the senses closed to the objective world.

The third and last thing to do is to *experience in your imagination what you would experience in reality had you achieved your goal.* Imagine that you possess a quality or something you desire which hitherto has not been yours. Surrender yourself completely to this feeling until your whole being is possessed by it. This state differs from reverie in this respect: it is the result of a *controlled imagination and a steadied concentrated attention*, whereas reverie is the result of an uncontrolled imagination—usually just a daydream. In the controlled state, a minimum of effort suffices to keep your consciousness filled with the feeling of the wish fulfilled. The physical and mental immobility of this state is a powerful aid to voluntary attention and a major factor of minimum effort.

The application of these three points:

> *Desire*
>
> *Physical immobility*
>
> *The assumption of the wish already fulfilled.*

is the way to at-one-ment or *union with your objective.*

One of the most prevalent misunderstandings is that this law works only for those having a devout or a religious objective. This is a fallacy. It works just as impersonally as the law of electricity works. It can be used for greedy, selfish purposes as well as noble ones. But it should always be borne in mind that ignoble thoughts and actions inevitably result in unhappy consequences.

20

RIGHTEOUSNESS

In the preceding chapter righteousness was defined as the *consciousness of already being what you want to be.* This is the true psychological meaning and obviously does not refer to adherence to moral codes, civil law or religious precepts. You cannot attach too much importance to being righteous.

In fact, the entire Bible is permeated with admonition and exhortations on this subject.

> *"Break off thy sins by righteousness."*
>
> DAN. 4:27

> *"My righteousness I hold fast, and will not let it go: my heart shall not reproach me so long as I live."*
>
> JOB 27:6

> *"My righteousness shall answer for me in time to come."*
>
> GENESIS 30:33

Very often the words "sin" and "righteousness" are used in the same quotation. This is a logical contrast of opposites and becomes enormously significant in the light of the psychological meaning of righteousness and the psychological meaning of sin. Sin means *to miss the mark*. Not to attain your desire, not to be the person you want to be is sinning. Righteousness is the consciousness of already being what you want to be. It is a changeless educative law that effects must follow causes. Only by righteousness can you be saved from sinning.

There is a widespread misunderstanding as to what it means to be "saved from sin". The following example will suffice to demonstrate this misunderstanding and to establish the truth. A person living in abject poverty may believe that by means of some religious or philosophical activity he can be "saved from sin" and his life improved as a result. If, however, he continues to live in the same state of poverty it is obvious that what he believed was not the truth, and, in fact, he was not "saved". On the other hand he can be saved by *righteousness*. The successful use of the law of assumption would have the inevitable result of an actual change in his life. He would no longer live in poverty. He would no longer miss the mark. He would be *saved from sin*.

> "*Except your righteousness shall exceed the righteousness of the scribes and Pharisees, ye shall in no wise enter into the kingdom of heaven.*"
>
> MATT. 5:20

Scribes and Pharisees mean those who are influenced and governed by the outer appearances—the rules and customs of the society in which they live, the vain desire to be thought well of by other men. Unless this state of mind is exceeded, your life will be one of limitation—of failure to attain your desires—of missing the mark—of sin. This righteousness is exceeded by *true righteousness* which is always the consciousness of *already being* that which you want to be.

One of the greatest pitfalls in attempting to use the law of assumption is focusing your attention on *things*, on a new home, a better job, a bigger bank balance. This is not the righteousness without which you "die in your sins." Righteousness is not the *thing* itself; *it is the consciousness, the feeling of already being the person you want to be, of already having the thing you desire.*

> *"Seek ye first the kingdom of God, and his*
> *righteousness; and all these things shall be added*
> *unto you."*
>
> MATTHEW 6:33

The kingdom (entire creation) of God (your I AM) is within you. Righteousness is the awareness that you *already* possess it all.

21

FREE WILL

The question is often asked, "what should be done between the assumption of the wish fulfilled and its realization?" *Nothing.* It is a delusion that, other than assuming the feeling of the wish fulfilled you can do anything to aid the realization of your desire. You think that you can do something, you want to do something; but, actually you can do nothing. *The illusion of the free will to do is but ignorance of the law of assumption* upon which all action is based. Everything happens automatically. All that befalls you, all that is done by you—*happens.* Your assumptions, *conscious or unconscious,* direct all thought and action to their fulfillment. To understand the law of assumption, to be convinced of its truth, means getting rid of all the illusions about free will to act. Free will actually means *freedom to select any idea you desire.* By assuming the idea *already* to be a fact, it is converted into reality. Beyond that, *free will ends* and everything happens in harmony with the concept assumed.

> "I can of mine ownself do nothing . . . because I seek not
> mine own will, but the will of the Father which hath
> sent me."

In this quotation the Father obviously refers to God. In an earlier chapter, God is defined as I AM. Since creation is finished, the Father is never in a position of saying *"I will be."* In other words, everything exists and the infinite I AM consciousness can speak only in the *present tense*.

> *"Not my will but thine be done."*

"I will be" is a confession that *"I am not"*. The Father's will is *always* "I AM". Until you realize that YOU are the Father (there is only one I AM and your infinite self is that I AM) your will is always *"I will be."*

In the law of assumption your *consciousness of being* is the Father's will. The mere wish without this consciousness is the "my will". This great quotation, so little understood, is a perfect statement of the law of assumption.

It is impossible to *do* anything. You must *be* in order to do.

If you had a different concept of yourself, everything would be different. You are *what you are*, so everything *is as it is*. The events which you observe are determined by the concept you have of yourself. If you change your concept of yourself, the events ahead of you in time are altered, but, thus altered, they *form again a deterministic sequence* starting from the moment of this changed concept. You are a being with powers of intervention, which enable you, by a change of consciousness, to alter the course of observed events—in fact, to *change your future*.

Deny the evidence of the senses, and assume the feeling of the wish fulfilled. Inasmuch as your assumption is *creative* and forms an atmosphere, your assumption, if it be a noble one, increases your assurance and helps you to reach a higher level of being. If, on the other hand, your assumption be an unlovely one, it hinders you and makes your downward way swifter. Just as the lovely assumptions create a harmonious atmosphere, so the hard and bitter feelings create a hard and bitter atmosphere.

> *"Whatsoever things are pure, just, lovely, of good report, think on these things."*

This means to make your assumptions the highest, noblest, happiest concepts. There is no better time to start than *now*. The present moment is always the most opportune in which to eliminate all unlovely assumptions and to concentrate only on the good. As well as yourself, claim for others their Divine inheritance. See only their good and the good in them. Stir the highest in others to confidence and self-assertion, by your sincere assumption of their good and you will be their prophet and their healer, for an inevitable fulfillment awaits all sustained assumptions.

You win by assumption what you can never win by force. An assumption is a certain motion of consciousness. This motion, like all motion, exercises an influence on the surrounding substance causing it to take the shape of, echo, and reflect the assumption. A change of fortune is a new direction and outlook, merely a change in arrangement of the same mind substance—*consciousness*.

If you would change your life, you must begin at the very source *with your own basic concept of self.* Outer change, becoming part of organizations, political bodies, religious bodies, is not enough. The cause goes deeper. The essential change must take place *in yourself,* in your own concept of self. You must assume that you are what you want to be and continue therein, for the *reality of your assumption has its being in complete independence of objective fact,* and will clothe itself in flesh if you persist in the feeling of the wish fulfilled. When you know that assumptions, if persisted in, harden into facts, then events which seem to the uninitiated mere accidents will be understood by you to be the logical and inevitable *effects* of your assumption.

The important thing to bear in mind is that you have *infinite free will in choosing your assumptions,* but no power to determine conditions and events. *You can create nothing, but your assumption determines what portion of creation you will experience.*

22

PERSISTENCE

*"And He said unto them, Which of you shall have
a friend, and shall go unto him at midnight, and
say unto him, Friend, lend me three loaves; for a
friend of mine in his journey is come to me, and I
have nothing to set before him? and he from within
shall answer and say, Trouble me not: the door is
now shut, and my children are with me in bed; I
cannot rise and give thee. I say unto you, Though he
will not rise and give him, because he is his friend,
yet because of his importunity he will rise and give
him as many as he needeth. And I say unto you,
Ask, and it shall be given you; seek, and ye shall
find; knock, and it shall be opened unto you."*

LUKE 11:5-9

There are three principle characters in this quotation; you and
the two friends mentioned. The first friend is a *desired state of consciousness*. The second friend is a *desire seeking fulfillment*. Three
is the symbol of wholeness, completion. Loaves symbolize substance. The shut door symbolizes the senses which separate the

seen from the unseen. Children in bed means ideas that are dormant. Inability to rise means a desired state of consciousness cannot rise to you, you must rise to it. Importunity means demanding persistency, a kind of brazen impudence. *Ask, seek* and *knock mean assuming the consciousness of already having what you desire.*

Thus the scriptures tell you that you must persist in rising to (assuming) the consciousness of your wish already being fulfilled. The promise is definite that if you are shameless in your impudence in assuming that you *already have that which your senses deny, it shall be given unto you—your desire shall be attained.*

The Bible teaches the necessity of persistence by the use of many stories. When Jacob sought a blessing from the Angel with whom he wrestled, he said

"I will not let thee go, except thou bless me."

When the Shunammite sought the help of Elisha, she said,

"As the Lord liveth, and as thy soul liveth, I will not leave thee, and he arose and followed her."

The same idea is expressed in another passage.

"And he spake a parable unto them that men ought always to pray, and not to faint; saying, There was in a city a judge, which feared not God, neither regarded man, and there was a widow in that city; and she came

unto him, saying Avenge me of mine adversary. And
he would not for a while; but afterward he said within
himself, Though I fear not God, nor regard man; yet
because this widow troubleth me, I will avenge her, lest
she weary me by her continual coming."

LUKE 18:1-5

The basic truth underlying each of these stories is that desire springs from the awareness of ultimate attainment and that persistence in maintaining the consciousness of the desire already being fulfilled results in its fulfillment.

It is not enough to feel yourself into the state of the answered prayer; you must persist in that state. That is the reason for the injunction 'man ought always to pray and not to faint'; here, *to pray means to give thanks for already having what you desire.* Only persistency in the assumption of the wish fulfilled can cause those subtle changes in your mind which result in the desired change in your life. It matters not whether they be "Angels", "Elisha" or "reluctant judges"; all *must* respond in harmony with your persistent assumption. When it appears that people other than yourself in your world do not act toward you as you would like, it is not due to reluctance on their part but a lack of *persistence* in your assumption of your life already being as you want it to be. Your assumption to be effective cannot be a single isolated act; it must be a maintained attitude of the wish fulfilled.

23

CASE HISTORIES

It will be extremely helpful at this point to cite a number of specific examples of the successful application of this law. *Actual case histories are given.* In each of these the problem is clearly defined and the way imagination was used to attain the required state of consciousness is fully described. In each of these instances the author of this book was either personally concerned or was told the facts by the person involved.

1

This is a story with every detail of which I am personally familiar.

In the spring of 1943 a recently drafted soldier was stationed in a large army camp in Louisiana. He was intensely eager to get out of the army but only in an entirely honorable way.

The only way he could do this was to apply for a discharge. The application then required the approval of his commanding officer to become effective. Based on army regulations, the decision of the commanding officer was final and could not be appealed. The soldier, following all the necessary procedure applied for a discharge. Within four hours his application was returned—marked "disapproved." Convinced he could not appeal the decision to any higher authority, military or civilian, he turned within to his own consciousness, determined to rely on the law of assumption.

The soldier realized that his consciousness was the only reality, that his particular state of consciousness determined the events he would encounter.

That night, in the interval between getting into bed and falling asleep, he concentrated on consciously using the law of assumption. *In imagination* he felt himself to be in his own apartment in New York City. He visualized his apartment, that is, in his mind's eye he actually saw his own apartment, mentally picturing each one of the familiar rooms with all the furnishings vividly real.

With this picture clearly visualized, and lying flat on his back, he completely relaxed physically. In this way he induced a state bordering on sleep at the same time retaining control of the direction of his attention. When his body was completely immobilized, he *assumed* that he was in his own room and felt himself to be lying in his own bed—a very different feeling from that of lying on an army cot. In imagination he rose from the bed, walked from room to room touching various pieces of furniture. He then went to the window and with his hands resting on the sill looked out on the street on which his apartment faced. *So vivid was all this in his imagination* that he saw in detail the pavement, the railings, the trees and the familiar red brick of the building on the opposite side of the street. He then returned to his bed and felt himself drifting off to sleep. He knew that it was most important in the successful use of this law that at the actual point of falling asleep his consciousness be filled with the assumption that he was already what he wanted to be. All that he did in imagination was based on the assumption that he was no longer in the army. Night after night the soldier enacted this drama. Night after night in imagination he felt himself, honorably discharged, back in his home seeing all the familiar surroundings and falling asleep in his own bed. This continued for eight nights. For eight days his *objective* experience continued to be directly opposite to his *subjective* experience in consciousness each night, before going to sleep. On the *ninth day* orders came through from Battalion headquarters for the soldier to fill out a new application for his discharge. Shortly after this was done he was ordered to report to the Colonel's office. During the discussion the Colonel asked him if he was still desirous of getting out of the army. Upon receiving an affirmative reply the Colonel said that he personally disagreed and while he had strong objections to approving of the discharge, he had decided to overlook these objections and to approve it. Within a few hours the application was approved and the soldier, now a civilian, was on a train bound for home.

2

This is a striking story of an extremely successful business man demonstrating the power of imagination and the law of assumption. I know this family intimately and all the details were told to me by the son described herein.

The story begins when he was twenty years old. He was next to the oldest in a large family of nine brothers and one sister. The father was one of the partners in a small merchandising business.

In his eighteenth year the brother referred to in this story left the country in which they lived and traveled two thousand miles to enter college and complete his education. Shortly after his first year in college he was called home because of a tragic event in connection with his father's business. Through the machinations of his associates, the father was not only forced out of his business, but was the object of false accusations impugning his character and integrity. At the same time he was deprived of his rightful share in the equity of the business. The result was he found himself largely discredited and almost penniless. It was under these circumstances that the son was called home from college.

He returned, his heart filled with one great resolution. He was determined that he would become outstandingly successful in business. The first thing he and his father did was to use the little money they had to start their own business. They rented a small store on a side street not far from the large business of which the father had been one of the principal owners. There they started a business bent upon real service to the community. It was shortly after that the son with instinctive awareness that it was bound to work, deliberately used imagination to attain an almost fantastic objective.

Every day on the way to and from work he passed the building of his father's former business—the biggest business of its kind in the country. It was one of the largest buildings with the most prominent location in the heart of the city. On the outside of the building was a huge sign on which the name of the firm was painted in large bold letters. Day after day as he passed by a great dream took shape in the son's mind. He thought of how wonderful it would be if it was his family that had this great building—his family that owned and operated this great business.

One day as he stood gazing at the building, *in his imagination* he saw a completely different name on the huge sign across the entrance. Now the large letters spelled out *his family name* (in these case histories actual names are not used. For the sake of clarity in this story we will use hypothetical names and assume that the son's family name was Lordard) where the sign read F. N. Moth & Co., *in imagination* he actually saw the name letter by letter, J. N. Lordard & Sons. He remained looking at the sign with his eyes wide open *imagining* that it read J. N. Lordard & Sons. Twice a day, week after week, month after month for two years he saw his family name over the front of that building. He was convinced that if he *felt strongly enough* that a thing was true it was bound to be the case, and by *seeing in imagination* his family name on the sign—which implied that they owned the business—he became convinced that one day they *would* own it.

During this period he told only one person what he was doing. He confided in his mother who with loving concern tried to discourage him in order to protect him from what might be a great disappointment. Despite this he persisted day after day. *Two years later the large company failed and the coveted building was up for sale.* On the day of the sale he seemed no nearer ownership than he had been two years before when he began to apply the law of assumption. During this period they had worked hard, and their customers had implicit confidence in them. However, they had not earned anything like the amount of money required for the purchase of the property. Nor did they have any source from which they could borrow the necessary capital. Making even more remote their chance of getting it was the fact that this was regarded as the most desirable property in the city and a number of wealthy business people were prepared to buy it. *On the actual day of the sale, to their complete surprise, a man, almost a total stranger, came into their shop and offered to buy the property for them.* (Due to some unusual conditions involved in this transaction the son's family could not even make a bid for the property.) They thought the man was joking. However, this was not the case. The man explained that he had watched them for some time, admired their ability, believed in their integrity and that supplying the capital for them to go into business on a large scale was an extremely sound investment for him. *That very day the property was theirs.* What the son had persisted in seeing in his imagination was now a reality. The hunch of the stranger was more than justified. Today this family owns not only the particular business referred to but owns many of the largest industries in the country in which they live.

The son, *seeing his family name over the entrance of this great building, long before it was actually there, was using exactly the technique that produces results. By assuming the feeling that he already had what he desired—by making this a vivid reality in his imagination—by determined persistence, regardless of appearance or circumstance, he inevitably caused his dream to become a reality.*

3

This is the story of a very unexpected result of an interview with a lady who came to consult me.

One afternoon a young grandmother, a business woman in New York, came to see me. She brought along her nine year old grandson who was visiting her from his home in Pennsylvania. In response to her questions, I explained the law of assumption describing in detail the procedure to be followed in attaining an objective. The boy sat quietly, apparently absorbed in a small toy truck while I explained to the grandmother the method of assuming the state of consciousness that would be hers were her desire already fulfilled. I told her the story of the soldier in camp who each night fell asleep, imagining himself to be in his own bed in his own home.

When the boy and his grandmother were leaving he looked up at me with great excitement and said, "I know what I want and, now, I know how to get it." Surprised, I asked him what it was he wanted; he told me he had his heart set on a puppy. To this the grandmother vigorously protested, telling the boy that it had been made clear repeatedly that he could not have a dog under any circumstances that his father and mother would not allow it, that the boy was too young to care for it properly and furthermore the father had a deep dislike for dogs—he actually hated to have one around.

All these were arguments the boy passionately desirous of having a dog, refused to understand. "Now I know what to do," he said. "Every night just as I am going off to sleep I am going to pretend that I have a dog and we are going for a walk." "No," said the grandmother, "that is not what Mr. Neville means. This was not meant for you. You cannot have a dog."

Approximately six weeks later the grandmother told me, what was to her, an astonishing story. The boy's desire to own a dog was so intense that he had absorbed all that I had told his grandmother of how to attain one's desire—and he believed implicitly that at last he knew how to get a dog.

Putting this belief into practice, *for many nights the boy imagined a dog was lying in his bed beside him. In imagination he petted the dog actually feeling its fur.* Things like playing with the dog and taking it for a walk filled his mind. Within a few weeks it happened. A newspaper in the city in which the boy lived, organized a special program in connection with Kindness to Animals week. All school children were requested to write an essay on "Why I Would Like to Own a Dog."

After entries from all the schools were submitted and judged, the winner of the contest was announced. The very same boy who weeks before in my apartment in New York had told me "Now I know how to get a dog" was the winner. In an elaborate ceremony, which was publicized with stories and pictures in the newspaper, the boy was awarded a beautiful *collie* puppy.

In relating this story the grandmother told me that if the boy had been given the money with which to buy a dog, the parents would have refused to do so and would have used it to buy a bond for the boy or put it in the savings bank for him. Furthermore, if someone had made the boy a gift of a dog, they would have refused it or given it away. But the dramatic manner in which the boy got the dog, the way he won the city-wide contest, the stories and pictures in the newspaper, the pride of achievement and joy of the boy himself all combined to bring about a change of heart in the parents, and they found themselves doing that which they never conceived possible—they allowed him to keep the dog.

All this the grandmother explained to me, and she concluded by saying that there was one particular kind of dog on which the boy had set his heart. *It was a Collie.*

4

This was told by the Aunt in the story to the entire audience at the conclusion of one of my lectures.

During the question period following my lecture on the law of assumption, a lady who had attended many lectures and had had personal consultation with me on a number of occasions, rose and asked permission to tell a story illustrating how she had successfully used the law.

She said that upon returning home from the lecture the week before, she had found her niece distressed and terribly upset. The husband of the niece, who was an officer in the Army Air Force stationed in Atlantic City, had just been ordered, along with the rest of his unit, to active duty in Europe. She tearfully told her Aunt that the reason she was upset was that she had been hoping her husband would be assigned to Florida as an Instructor. They both loved Florida and were anxious to be stationed there and not to be separated. Upon hearing this story the aunt stated that there was only one thing to do and that was to apply immediately the law of assumption. "Let's actualize it," she said. "If you were actually in Florida, what would you do? You would feel the warm breeze. You would smell the salt air. You would feel your toes sinking down into the sand. Well, let's do all that right now."

They took off their shoes and turning out the lights, *in imagination they felt themselves actually in Florida feeling the warm breeze, smelling the sea air, pushing their toes into the sand.*

Forty-eight hours later the husband received a change of orders. His new instructions were to report immediately to Florida as an Air Force Instructor. Five days later his wife was on a train to join him. While the Aunt, in order to help her niece to attain her desire, joined in with the niece in assuming the state of consciousness required, *she* did not go to Florida. That was not her desire. On the other hand, that was the *intense longing* of the niece.

5

This case is especially interesting because of the short interval of time between the application of this law of assumption and its visible manifestation.

A very prominent woman came to me in deep concern. She maintained a lovely city apartment and a large country home; but because the many demands made upon her were greater than her modest income, it was absolutely essential that she rent her apartment if she and her family were to spend the summer at their country home.

In previous years the apartment had been rented without difficulty early in the spring, but the day she came to me the rental season for summer sublets was over. The apartment had been in the hands of the best real estate agents for months, but no one had been interested even in coming to see it.

When she had described her predicament I explained how the law of assumption could be brought to bear on solving her problem. I suggested that by imagining the apartment had been rented by a person desiring immediate occupancy and by assuming that this was the case, her apartment actually would be rented. In order to create the necessary feeling of naturalness—the feeling that it was already a fact that her apartment was rented, I suggested that she drift off into sleep that very night imagining herself, *not in her apartment*, but in whatever place she would sleep were the apartment suddenly rented. She quickly grasped the idea and said that in such a situation she would sleep in her country home even though it were not yet opened for the summer.

This interview took place on Thursday. At nine o'clock the following Saturday morning she phoned me from her home in the country—excited and happy. She told me that on Thursday night *she had fallen asleep actually imagining and feeling that she was sleeping in her other bed in her country home many miles away from the city apartment she was occupying.* On Friday, the very next day, a highly desirable tenant, one who met all her requirements as a responsible person, not only rented the apartment but rented it on the condition that he could move in that very day.

6

Only the most complete and intense use of the law of assumption could have produced such results in this extreme situation.

Four years ago a friend of our family asked that I talk with his twenty-eight year old son who was not expected to live.

He was suffering from a rare heart disease. This disease resulted in a disintegration of the organ. Long and costly medical care had been of no avail. Doctors held out no hope for recovery. For a long time the son had been confined to his bed. His body had shrunk to almost a skeleton, and he could talk and breathe only with great difficulty. His wife and two small children were home when I called and his wife was present throughout our discussion.

I started by telling him that there was only one solution to any problem and that solution was a change of attitude. Since talking exhausted him, I asked him to nod in agreement if he understood clearly what I said. This he agreed to do. I described the facts underlying the law of consciousness—in fact that consciousness was the only reality. I told him that the way to change any condition was to change his state of consciousness concerning it. As a specific aid in helping him to assume the feeling of already being well, I suggested that in *imagination, he see the doctor's face express-ing incredulous amazement in finding him recovered, contrary to all reason, from the last stages of an incurable disease, that he see him double checking in his examination and hear him saying over and over,* "It's a miracle—it's a miracle."

He not only understood all this clearly but he believed it implicitly. He promised that he would faithfully follow this procedure. His wife who had been listening intently assured me that she, too, would diligently use the law of assumption and her imagination in the same way as her husband. The following day I sailed for New York—all this taking place during a winter vacation in the tropics.

Several months later I received a letter saying the son had made a miraculous recovery. On my next visit I met him in person. He was in perfect health, actively engaged in business and thoroughly enjoying the many social activities of his friends and family.

He told me that from the day I left he never had any doubt that "it" would work. He described how he had faithfully followed the suggestion I had made to him and *day after day had lived completely in the assumption of already being well and strong.*

Now, four years after his recovery, he is convinced that the only reason he is here today is due to his successful use of the law of assumption.

7

This story illustrates the successful use of the law by a New York business executive.

In the fall of 1950 an executive of one of New York's prominent banks discussed with me a serious problem with which he was confronted. He told me that the outlook for his personal progress and advancement was very dim. Having reached middle age and feeling that a marked improvement in position and income was justified, he had "talked it out" with his superiors. They frankly told him that any major improvement was impossible and intimated that if he was dissatisfied he could seek another job. This, of course, only increased his uneasiness. In our talk he explained that he had no great desire for really big money but that he had to have a substantial income in order to maintain his home comfortably and to provide for the education of his children in good preparatory schools and colleges. This he found impossible on his present income. The refusal of the bank to assure him of any advancement in the near future resulted in a feeling of discontent and an intense desire to secure a better position with considerably more money. He confided in me that the kind of job he would like better than anything in the world was one in which he managed the investment funds of a large institution such as a foundation or great university.

In explaining the law of assumption, I stated that his present situation was only a manifestation of his concept of himself, and declared that if he wanted to change the circumstances in which he found himself, he could do so by changing his concept of himself. In order to bring about this change of consciousness, and thereby a change in his situation, I asked him to follow this procedure every night just before he fell asleep. *In imagination he was to feel that he was retiring at the end of one of the most important and successful days of his life. He was to imagine that he had actually closed a deal that very day to join the kind of organization he yearned to be with and in exactly the capacity he wanted.* I suggested to him that if he succeeded in completely filling his mind with this feeling, he would experience a definite sense of relief. In this mood his uneasiness and discontent would be a thing of the past. He would feel the contentment that comes with the fulfillment of desire. I wound up by assuring him that if he did this faithfully he would inevitably get the kind of position he wanted.

This was the first week of December. *Night after night without exception he followed this procedure.* Early in February a director of one of the wealthiest foundations in the world asked this executive if he would be interested in joining the foundation in an executive capacity handling investments. After some brief discussion he accepted.

Today at a substantially higher income and with the assurance of steady progress, this man is in a position far exceeding all that he had hoped for.

8

The man and wife in this story have attended my lectures for a number of years. It is an interesting illustration of the conscious use of this law by two people concentrating on the same objective at one time.

This man and wife were an exceptionally devoted couple. Their life was completely happy and entirely free from any problems or frustrations.

For sometime they had planned to move into a larger apartment. The more they thought about it the more they realized that what they had their hearts set on was a beautiful penthouse. In discussing it together the husband explained that he wanted one with a huge window looking out on a magnificent view. The wife said she would like to have one side of the walls mirrored from top to bottom. They both wanted to have a wood-burning fire place. It was a 'must' that the apartment be in New York City.

For months they had searched for just such an apartment in vain. In fact, the situation in the city was such that the securing of any kind of apartment was almost an impossibility. They were so scarce that not only were there waiting lists for them but all sorts of special deals including premiums, the buying of furniture, etc., were involved. New apartments were being leased long before they were completed, many being rented from the blue prints of the building.

Early in the spring after months of fruitless seeking, they finally located one which they seriously considered. It was a penthouse apartment in a building just being completed on upper Fifth Avenue facing Central Park. It had one serious drawback. Being a new building it was not subject to rent control and the couple felt the yearly rental was exorbitant. In fact, it was several thousand dollars a year more than they had considered paying. During the spring months of March and April they continued looking at various penthouses throughout the city but they always came back to this one. Finally they decided to increase the amount they would pay substantially and made a proposition which the agent for the building agreed to forward to the owners for consideration.

It was at this point, without discussing it with each other, each determined to apply the law of assumption. It was not until later that each learned what the other had done. *Night after night, they both fell asleep in imagination in the apartment they were considering. The husband, lying with his eyes closed, would imagine that his bedroom windows were overlooking the park. He would imagine going to the window the first thing in the morning and enjoying the view. He felt himself sitting on the terrace overlooking the park, having cocktails with his wife and friends, all thoroughly enjoying it. He filled his mind with actually feeling himself in the penthouse and on the terrace. During all this time, unknown to him, his wife was doing the same thing.*

Several weeks went by without any decision on the part of the owners but they continued to imagine as they fell asleep each night that they were actually sleeping in the penthouse.

One day, to their complete surprise, one of the employees in the apartment building in which they lived told them that the penthouse there was vacant. They were astonished because theirs was one of the most desirable buildings in the city with a perfect location right on Central Park. They knew there was a long waiting list of people trying to get an apartment in their building. The fact that a penthouse had unexpectedly become available was kept quiet by the management because they were not in a position to consider any applicants for it. Upon learning that it was vacant this couple immediately made a request that it be rented to them, only to be told that this was impossible. The fact was that not only were there several people on a waiting list for a penthouse in the building but it was actually promised to one family. Despite this the couple had a series of meetings with the management, at the conclusion of which the apartment was theirs.

The building being subject to rent control their rental was just about what they had planned to pay when they first started looking for a penthouse. The location, the apartment itself, and the large terrace surrounding it on the South, West and North was beyond all their expectations—and in the living room on one side is a giant window 15 feet by 8 feet with a magnificent view of Central Park; one wall is mirrored from floor to ceiling and there is a wood-burning fireplace.

24

FAILURE

This book would not be complete without some discussion of *failure* in the attempted use of the law of assumption. It is entirely possible that you either have had or will have a number of failures in this respect—many of them in really important matters. If, having read this book, having a thorough knowledge of the application and working of the law of assumption, you faithfully apply it in an effort to attain some intense desire and fail, what is the reason? If to the question, did you persist enough?, you can answer yes—and still the attainment of your desire was not realized, what is the reason for failure?

The answer to this is the most important factor in the successful use of the law of assumption. *The time it takes your assumption to become fact, your desire to be fulfilled, is directly proportionate to the naturalness of your feeling of already being what you want to be—of already having what you desire.*

The fact that it does not feel *natural* to you to be what you imagine yourself to be is *the secret of your failure*. Regardless of your desire, regardless of how faithfully and intelligently you follow the law if you do not feel *natural* about what you want to be *you will not be it*. If it does not feel natural to you to get a better job you will not get a better job. The whole principle is vividly expressed by the Bible phrase "you die in your sins"—you do not transcend from your present level to the state desired.

How can this feeling of naturalness be achieved? The secret lies in one word—*imagination*. For example, this is a very simple illustration. Assume that you are securely chained to a large heavy iron bench. You could not possibly run, in fact you could not even walk. In these circumstances it would not be natural for you to run. You could not even *feel* that it was natural for you to run. But you could easily *imagine* yourself running. In that instant, while your consciousness is filled with your *imagined* running, you have forgotten that you are bound. In *imagination* your running was completely natural.

The essential feeling of naturalness can be achieved by *persistently filling your consciousness with imagination*—imagining yourself being what you want to be or having what you desire.

Progress can spring only from your imagination, from your desire to transcend your present level. What you truly and literally *must* feel is that *with your imagination, all things are possible*. You must realize that changes are not caused by caprice, but by a change of consciousness. You may fail to achieve or sustain the particular state of consciousness necessary to produce the effect you desire. But, once you know that consciousness is the only reality and is the sole creator of your particular world and have burnt this truth into your whole being, then you know that success or failure is entirely in your own hands. Whether or not you are disciplined enough to sustain the required state of consciousness in specific instances has no bearing on the truth of the law itself—that an assumption, if persisted in, will harden into fact. The certainty of the truth of this law must remain despite great disappointment and tragedy—even when you "see the light of life go out and all the world go on as though it were still day." You must not believe that because your assumption failed to materialize, the truth that assumptions do materialize is a lie. If your assumptions are not fulfilled it is because of some error or weakness in your consciousness. However, these errors and weaknesses *can be overcome*. Therefore, press on to the attainment of ever higher levels by feeling that you *already are* the person you want to be. And remember that the time it takes your assumption to become reality is *proportionate to the naturalness of being it.*

> *"Man surrounds himself with the true image of*
> *himself. Every spirit builds itself a house and beyond*
> *its house a world, and beyond its world a heaven.*
> *Know then that the world exists for you. For you the*
> *phenomenon is perfect. What we are, that only can*
> *we see. All that Adam had, all that Caesar could, you*
> *have and can do. Adam called his house, heaven and*
> *earth. Caesar called his house, Rome; you perhaps call*
> *yours a cobbler's trade; a hundred acres of land, or a*
> *scholar's garret. Yet line for line and point for point,*
> *your dominion is as great as theirs, though without fine*

name. Build therefore your own world. As fast as you conform your life to the pure idea in your mind, that will unfold its great proportion."

EMERSON

25

FAITH

*"A miracle is the name given, by those who
have no faith, to the works of faith."*

*"Faith is the substance of things hoped for, the evidence
of things not seen."*

HEB. 11:1

The very reason for the law of assumption is contained in this quotation. If there were not a deep seated awareness that that which you hope for had substance and was possible of attainment it would be impossible to assume the consciousness of being or having it. It is the fact that *creation is finished and everything exists that stirs you to hope*—and hope, in turn, *implies expectation*, and without expectation of success it would be impossible to use consciously the law of assumption. "Evidence" is a sign of actuality. Thus, this quotation means that *faith is the awareness of the reality of that which you assume.* Consequently, it is obvious that a lack of faith means disbelief in the existence of that which you desire. Inasmuch as that which you experience is the faithful reproduction of your state of consciousness, lack of faith will mean perpetual failure in any *conscious* use of the law of assumption.

In all the ages of history faith has played a major role. It permeates all the great religions of the world, it is woven all through mythology and yet, today, it is almost universally misunderstood.

Contrary to popular opinion, the efficacy of faith is not due to the work of any outside agency. It is from first to last *an activity of your own consciousness.*

The Bible is full of many statements about faith, the true meaning of which few are aware. Here are some typical examples:

> *"Unto us was the gospel preached, as well as unto*
> *them: but the word preached did not profit them, not*
> *being mixed with faith in them that heard it."*
>
> HEB. 4:2

In this quotation the 'us' and 'them' make clear that all of us hear the gospel. "Gospel" means good news. Very obviously good news for you would be that you had attained your desire. This is always being 'preached' to you by your infinite self. To hear that which you desire does exist and you need only to accept it in consciousness is good news. Not "mixing with faith" means to deny the reality of that which you desire. Hence there is no "profit" (attainment) possible.

"O faithless and perverse generation, how long shall I
be with you."

The meaning of "faithless" has been made clear. "Perverse" means turned the wrong way, in other words, the consciousness of *not* being what you want to be. To be faithless, that is, to disbelieve in the reality of that which you assume, is to be perverse. "How long shall I be with you" means that the fulfillment of your desire is *predicated upon your change to the right state of consciousness*. It is just as though that which you desire is telling you that it will not be yours until you turn from being faithless and perverse to righteousness. As already stated, righteousness is the consciousness of already being what you want to be.

"By faith he forsook Egypt, not fearing the wrath of the
king: for he endured, as seeing him who is invisible."

HEB. 11:27

"Egypt" means darkness, belief in many gods (causes). The "king" symbolizes the power of outside conditions or circumstances. "He" is your concept of yourself as already being what you want to be. "Enduring as seeing him who is invisible" means persisting in the assumption that your desire is *already* fulfilled. Thus this quotation means that by persisting in the assumption that you already are the person you want to be you rise above all doubt, fear and belief in the power of outside conditions or circumstances; and your world inevitably conforms to your assumption.

The dictionary definitions of faith:

> *"the ascent of the mind or understanding to the truth;*
> *unwavering adherence to principle"*

are so pertinent that they might well have been written with the law of assumption in mind.

Faith does not question—Faith knows.

26

DESTINY

Your destiny is that which you must inevitably experience. Really it is an infinite number of individual destinies, each of which when attained is the starting place for a new destiny.

Since life is *infinite* the concept of an ultimate destiny is inconceivable. When we understand that consciousness is the only reality, we know that it is the only creator. This means that your consciousness is the creator of your destiny. The fact is, you are creating your destiny every moment, *whether you know it or not.* Much that is good and even wonderful has come into your life without you having any inkling that you were the creator of it.

However, the understanding of the causes of your experience, and the *knowledge that you are the sole creator of the contents of your life, both good and bad, not only make you a much keener observer of all phenomena but through the awareness of the power of your own consciousness, intensifies your appreciation of the richness and grandeur of life.*

Regardless of occasional experiences to the contrary it is *your destiny to rise to higher and higher states of consciousness, and to bring into manifestation more and more of creation's infinite wonders.* Actually you are destined to reach the point where you realize that through your own desire you can consciously create your successive destinies.

The study of this book, with its detailed exposition of consciousness and the operation of the law of assumption, is the master key to the conscious attainment of your highest destiny.

This very day start your new life. Approach every experience in a new frame of mind—with a new state of consciousness. Assume the noblest and the best for yourself in every respect and continue therein.

Make believe—great wonders are possible.

27

REVERENCE

*"Never wouldst Thou have made
anything if Thou hadst not loved it."*
WISDOM 11:24

In all creation, in all eternity, in all the realms of your infinite being the most wonderful fact is that which is stressed in the first chapter of this book. *You are God.* You are the "I am that I am." You are consciousness. You are the creator. This is the mystery, this is the great secret known by the seers, prophets and mystics throughout the ages. This is the truth that you can never know *intellectually*. Who is this you? That it is you, John Jones or Mary Smith is absurd. It is the *consciousness which knows* that you are John Jones or Mary Smith. It is your greater self, your deeper self, your infinite being. Call it what you will. The important thing is that *it is within you, it is you, it is your world*. It is this fact that underlies the immutable law of assumption. It is upon this fact that your very existence is built. It is this fact that is the foundation of every chapter of this book. No, you cannot know this intellectually, you cannot debate it, you cannot substantiate it. *You can only feel it. You can only be aware of it.*

Becoming aware of it, one great emotion permeates your being. You live with a perpetual feeling of *reverence*. The knowledge that your creator is the very self of yourself and never would have made you had he not *loved you* must fill your heart with devotion, yes, with adoration. One knowing glimpse of the world about you at any single instant of time is sufficient to fill you with profound awe and a feeling of worship.

It is when your feeling of reverence is most intense that you are closest to God and *when you are closest to God your life is richest.*

> *"Our deepest feelings are precisely those we*
> *are least able to express, and even in the act*
> *of adoration, silence is our highest praise."*

II

CHARIOT OF FIRE: THE IDEAS OF NEVILLE GODDARD

By Mitch Horowitz

This was my first public talk on Neville, delivered June 28, 2013, at the now-defunct arts space Observatory in Gowanus, Brooklyn. It includes the complete talk and the question-and-answer session that followed. —MH

S ome of you know my work, my book *Occult America*, and things that I've done related to that. *Occult America* is a history of supernatural religious movements in our country. A few of you who know my work are aware that I feel strongly that occult, esoteric, and metaphysical movements have touched this country very deeply. I write about these movements not only as a historian who is passionately interested in how the paranormal, occult, and supernatural have influenced our religion, our economy, our psychology, and our views of ourselves; but I also write about these things as a participant, as a kind of a believing historian. I do not view occult thought movements strictly as historical phenomena, which may reveal aspects of human nature; that's true enough, but I think that within the folds of such movements there exist actual ideas for human transformation.

I don't believe in looking into philosophies simply in order to place them in museum cases and to label them. Rather, I think we need practical philosophies that contribute to real-life transformation in the here and now. In my study of different occult and mystical systems, some of which I wrote about in *Occult America* and some of which I'm writing about in my next book *One Simple Idea*, I must tell you the most impactful, elegant, simplest, and dramatically powerful figure I have come across is Neville Goddard.

He was born to an Anglican family on the island of Barbados in 1905. It was a family of ten children, nine boys and one girl. Neville came here to New York City to study theater in 1922. He had some success and also fell into a variety of mystical and occult philosophies. Neville eventually came to feel that he had discovered the master key to existence. Up to this point in my experiments, I conclude: he may have been right.

You can determine that for yourself, because I'm going to start off this presentation by giving you his system. I am also going to provide some history: where he came from, who his teachers were, what his ideas grew out of, who he has influenced, and why he proved vastly ahead of his time. Some of the methods and ideas that Neville experimented with are being heard about today through unsensationalized discussions of developments in quantum physics and neurobiology.

I will also consider the possible identity of the hidden spiritual master named Abdullah who Neville said was his teacher in New York City. Are there spiritual masters, masters of wisdom in the world? Are there beings who can provide help to us when we sincerely desire it? Is that a real possibility or is that just fantasy? I think it's a possibility. It may have played out in his existence.

But we're really here to talk about the practical side of his philosophy. There are many interesting figures who I reference in this talk—dramatic figures whose lives spanned the globe. But we're talking about Neville *because of the usefulness of his ideas* and I want to start with that.

Mind as God

Neville believed very simply in the principle that your imagination is God, the human imagination is God, and that Scripture and all the stories from Scripture, both Old Testament and New Testament, have absolutely no basis in historical reality. The entire book is a metaphor, a blueprint for the individual's personal development. In particular, the New Testament tells the story of God symbolically, of God descending into human form, of humanity becoming asleep to its own divine essence or Christ essence, and believing itself to live within a coarse, limited world of material parameters, of then being crucified and experiencing the agony of his forgetfulness. Christ yells out in the across, "My God, my God, why hast thou forsaken me?" The individual is then resurrected into the realization of his or her divine potentiality, which is the birthright of every individual.

Neville maintained, through his reading of Scripture, his personal probing as a philosopher, and his experiments as an individual, that there is no God outside of the creative powers of the imagination; and that those who wrote Scripture never intended to communicate that there was a God outside of the individual's imagination. The creative force within us—which thinks, plans, pictures, ponders, and falls in and out of emotive states—is symbolically represented in Scripture as God.

Neville maintained that your thoughts, your mental pictures, and your emotive states create your concrete reality—and do at every moment of existence. We are oblivious and asleep to this fact. We live in these coarse shells, we suffer, we cry, we have fleeting joys, we leave these forms. We go through life in a state of slumber without ever knowing that each one of us is a physical form in which creation is experiencing itself. We eventually come to the realization through our causative minds we can experience the powers written about in symbolically in the New Testament and embodied as the story of Christ resurrected.

I want to say to you that Neville meant all of this in the most radical and literal sense. There was nothing inexact or qualified in what he said. He took a radical stand and he continually put up a challenge to his audiences: *try it*. Try it tonight and if it doesn't work, discard me, discard my philosophy, prove me a liar. He sold nothing. He published a handful of books, most of which are now public domain. He gave lectures Grateful Dead-style where he allowed everybody to tape record them and distribute them freely, which is why his talks are now all over the Internet. There's nothing to join. There's nothing to buy. There's no copyright holder. There's just this man and his ideas.

Three-Step Miracle

Neville's outlook can be reduced to a three-part formula, which is incredibly simple, but also requires commitment.

First, every creative act begins with an absolute, passionate desire. It sounds so easy, doesn't it? We walk around all day long with desires; I want this, I want that, I want money, I want relationships, I want this person to pay attention to me, I want this attainment. But look again. We often have superficial understandings of our desires and we're dishonest about our desires.

We're dishonest about our desires because we don't want to say to ourselves, in our innermost thoughts, *what we really want*. Sometimes we're repulsed by our desires, and that's the truth. We live in a society that's filled with so much personal license and freedom on the surface, of course, but we often don't want to acknowledge things to ourselves that maybe we believe aren't attractive.

I want to tell a personal story and I want to be very personal with you because I'm talking to you about a man and a philosophy that is enormously challenging and practical, if you really take it seriously. I have no right to be standing here talking to you unless I tell you about some of my own experiences. I want to tell you about one of my personal experiences as it relates to this first point: *desire*. Years ago, I knew a woman who was a psychic. A nationally known person, somebody I assume some of you have heard of, not household name maybe, but well known. I thought she had a genuine psychical gift. I thought she had something.

Yet I didn't like the way she led her life because I thought, personally, that she could be a violent person—not physically violent but emotionally; she would manipulate people around her, bully people, push people around. I didn't really like her but I did feel that she had a true gift. One night I was talking to her. We were on a parking lot somewhere having conversation, and she stopped. She said to me, "You know what you want? You want power. But your problem is that you have an overdeveloped super-ego." As soon as I heard this I wanted to push it away. And I spent years pushing it away. Years pushing it away because I thought to myself, "Well, I don't want power like you. I don't want power to push people around, to bully people, to be violent towards people. I don't want that, no." So I recoiled from what she said. But it haunted me. It haunted me. I could never get away from it.

You don't know really what haunts you until you confront something in yourself, or maybe something that a sensitive person says to you, which leaves the terrible impression that they might just may be speaking the truth. So when Neville talks about desire, he's not talking about something superficial that we keep telling ourselves day after day. He really wants you to get down into the guts of things, where you might want something that makes you very uncomfortable. There are ways we don't like to see ourselves. But Neville maintains that desire is the voice of the God within you; and to walk away from it is to walk away from the potential greatness within yourself. Desire is the language of God. Neville means this in the most literal sense.

The second step is physical immobility. This is the part where you actually do something. You enter a physically immobile state. Choose the time of day when you like to meditate, whether it's early morning, whether it's late at night. The time of day Neville chose was 3:00 p.m. He would finish lunch, settle into an easy chair, and go into a drowsy state. Now, this is very important because we think of meditation typically as a state of exquisite awareness. We don't think of meditation as drowsiness. People use these terms in different ways. Neville believed—and as I will talk about this later in this presentation—that the mind is uniquely powerful and suggestible in its drowsy state, hovering just before sleep, but not yet crossing into sleep. It is a controlled reverie. Or a cognizant dream state. Sleep researchers call this hypnagogia. You enter it twice daily: at night when you're drifting off and in the morning when you're coming to (this is sometimes called hypnopompia).

Our minds are exquisitely sensitive at such times. People who suffer from depression or grief describe their early morning hours as the most difficult time of day. The reason for that, I'm convinced, is that it is a time when our rational defenses are down. We're functioning almost entirely from emotion. We are conscious but we are also in this very subtle, fine state between sleep and wakefulness, and our rational defenses are slackened. Let me tell you something vital—and I can attest to this from personal experience. If you are trying to solve a personal problem, do not do it at 5:00 in the morning. Do not.

Your rational defenses are down when you need them most.

When you need your your intellect, whether you're solving a financial problem, whether you're going through a relationship problem, whatever it is, do not use the time of day when it is at its lowest ebb. At 5 a.m. your mind isn't fully working. Your emotions are working. It is a tough, tough time to deal with problems. But it is a very unique time to deal with desires—and for the same reason. When your rational defenses are down, your mind can go in remarkable directions.

I'm going to talk later about developments in psychical research, where there are some extraordinary findings under rigorous clinical conditions, in which people are induced into this hypnagogic state, the state between sleep and wakefulness, and the mind can evince remarkable abilities.

So, Neville said to enter this state of physical immobility. You can most easily do it just before you go to sleep at night. He didn't say do it when you wake up in the morning but I think you can extrapolate that that works, too. You can also do it when you're meditating. You can do it whenever you want. It takes only a few minutes, but go into a very relaxed bodily state or just let yourself be taken into it naturally when you go to bed at night.

And now *the third step*: form a very clear, simple mental scene that would naturally occur following the fulfilment of your desire. Keep it very simple. Run it through your head as long as it feels natural.

A woman attended one of Neville's lectures in Los Angeles and told him simply that she wanted to be married. He told her to enact the mental feeling of a wedding band on her finger. Just that. Keep it very simple. Mentally feel the weight and pressure of the ring on your finger. Maybe feel yourself spinning it around on your finger. Maybe there's something you want from an individual. Select an act that seems simple. Just a handshake, perhaps. Something that communicates that you received something—recognition, a promotion, a congratulation.

You must picture yourself *within* the scene. You must see from within the scene. Don't see yourself doing something as though you're watching it on a screen. Neville was adamant about this. He would say, "If I want to imagine myself climbing a ladder, I don't *see* myself climbing a ladder. *I climb.*" You must feel hands on the ladder. Feel your weight was you step up each rung. You are not watching the scene—you are in it.

Whatever it is, find one simple, clear, persuasive, physical action that would communicate the attainment of your goal, and think from that end, think from the end of the goal fulfilled. Run this through your mind as long as it feels natural.

Neville would always say, "When you open your eyes, you'll be back here in the coarse world that you might not want to be in, but if you persist in this, your assumption will harden into fact." You may wake up, come out of your physical immobility, and discover that the world remains exactly as it was. If you want to be in Paris and you open your eyes in New York, you may be disappointed. Keep doing it and extraordinary events will unfold to secure precisely what you have pictured in your mind. Persistence is key.

Using the Emotions

Now, I want to emphasize one aspect of Neville's philosophy, which I feel that he could have gone further in explaining, and that is the necessity of your visual scene being accompanied by the attendant emotional state. We often make the mistake in the positive-mind movement of equating thought with emotions. They are different things. I have a physical existence. I have intellectual existence. I have an emotional existence. Part of why you may feel torn apart when approaching mind causation is that all of these aspects of your existence—the physical, the mental, and the emotional— are going their own way, running on separate tracks. You may vow not to eat, and you may mean it, but the body wants to eat—and next thing you know the body is in control. You may vow not to get angry—but the emotions take over and you fly into rage. You may think, "I am going to use my intellect and not my passions"—but the passions rule your action. These three forces, body, mind, and intellect, have their own lives—and intellect is the weakest among them. Otherwise we wouldn't struggle with addictions or violent outbursts or impulsive actions. But we find that we are pieces.

This presents a challenge. Because when you enact your mental scene of fulfillment, you also must attain the emotive state that you would feel in your fulfillment. When you approach this teaching you benefit from being a kind of actor or thespian, as Neville was early in his career. Method Acting is a good exercise for enacting this method. Read Stanislavski's *An Actor Prepares*. Anybody who's been trained in Method Acting often learns to use a kind of inner monologue to get themselves into an emotional state. That's a good exercise. You must get the emotions in play.

Let's say you want a promotion at work. You could picture your boss saying to you, "Congratulations—well done!" You must try to feel the emotions that you would feel in that state. Hypnagogia can also help with this because, as noted, the rational defenses are lowered and the mind is more suggestible.

To review Neville's formula: 1) Identify an intense and sincere desire. 2) Enter a state of physical immobility, i.e., the drowsy hypnagogic state. 3) Gently run a scene through your mind that would occur if your wish was fulfilled. Let it be an emotional experience.

How It Happened

I want to tell another personal story. Neville always challenged his listeners: "Test it. Test it. What do you most desire right now? Go home this night and test it. Prove me wrong," he would say. I decided to test him and I want to give you the example. It is recent to this talk, explicit, and absolutely real.

In addition to being a writer, I'm a publisher. I'm the editor-in-chief of a division of Penguin that publishes New Age and metaphysical books. After considerable effort to locate the descendants of the author, I acquired the rights to republish a 1936 self-help book called *Wake Up and Live!* by Dorothea Brande. In this book, Brande writes that the pathology of human nature is what she called a *will to fail*. We fear failure and humiliation more than we crave success, so we constantly sabotage our plans in order to avoid the possibility of failure. We procrastinate. We make excuses. We blow important due dates or wreck professional relationships because we're more frightened of failure than we are hungry for success. But Brande further believed that if you were to *act as though it were impossible to fail*, you could bypass this self-negating pattern and achieve great things.

As mentioned, I spent a year trying to find her descendants so I could buy rights to this book, and I finally did. After this effort, I learned of an audio publisher who wanted to issue out an audio edition. I do a lot of audio narration, although I was still just getting started at this point, and I told this publisher that I was eager to narrate this book. I had recorded for this publisher before. It had been successful and I thought, naturally they'll agree. But they wouldn't get back to me. My e-mails were ignored. My phone calls were ignored. I was very frustrated. I couldn't understand why they wouldn't want me to do this book. I was obviously brimming of passion for it. I had done good work before. But I just couldn't get anywhere. I was totally stuck. I was very frustrated. Finally the publisher replied to me with a decisive, "No."

I thought to myself, "Well, not only do I want to be doing more audiobooks, but this is the kind of book that I was born to read." I went into this exercise and I formed a mental picture. I'm not going to tell you what it was. It was too personal but it was also very simple. I formed a mental picture. I reviewed it faithfully two or three times a day for about two weeks.

Out of the clear blue, without any outer intervention on my part, a rights manager called to say, "Guess what? Someone else actually just bought the rights to that book. It's not with that audio publisher anymore. There's been a change. There's a new audio publisher." I said, "Please tell that new publisher that I am dying to read this book." She got back to me. The new publisher said, "I sent Horowitz an e-mail a week ago asking him to read another audiobook and he never get back to me." I had gotten no such email. I went into my spam folder and found nothing. I went into a still deeper spam filter—and there is was. We signed a deal for me to narrate a total of three books, including *Wake Up and Live!*

I went from being ignored, to being told no, to signing a three-book narration deal. That relationship became one of the most central of my professional life. That same publisher issued this book that you are now reading. I did nothing to influence any of this in the outer world. I didn't do anything or contact anybody. I just did my visualization as Neville prescribed. It ended with the new audio publisher saying, "I contacted him a week ago. Why didn't he get back to me?"

For various reasons, this episode could be considered ordinary and I'm not oblivious to that. But I can say the following: from where I stood, and from long experience, it did not appear ordinary. "Take my challenge and put my words to the test. If the law does not work, its knowledge will not comfort you, and if it is not true, you must discard it. I hope you will be bold enough to test me" That's what Neville said over and over. You don't have to join anything. You don't have to buy anything. You can go online and listen to his lectures. Many of his books can be downloaded for free. His lectures can be downloaded for free. All he would insist is: "Put me to the test. Put me to the test."

Ecce Homo

Neville was born in 1905 on the island of Barbados, as mentioned. He was not born to a wealthy, land-holding family. He was born to an Anglican family of merchants. He was one of ten children, nine boys and a girl. The family ran a food service and catering business, which later mushroomed into a highly profitable corporation. One of the things that I found about Neville is that the life details and events he claimed in his lectures often turned out to be verifiably true.

I've done a lot of work to track down and verify some of Neville's claims. He came to New York City to study theater and dancing in 1922. He didn't have any money. He was a poor kid and knocked about. He lived in a shared apartment on the Upper West Side on West 75th Street. His large family back home was not rich but over the course of time, they became very rich. They later put him on kind of an allowance or a monthly stipend. Much later, he was able to pursue his studies into the occult, into philosophy, into mysticism, completely independently.

Goddard Industries is today a major catering business in Barbados. They not only cater parties and events, but they cater for airlines. They cater for cruise ships and industrial facilities. By the standards of the West Indies, they're a large and thriving business. Everything that was said in his lectures about his family's growth in fortune is true. His father, Joe or Joseph, founded the business. Neville talks frequently about his older brother Victor, in his lectures. I'm not going to go into all the details here because I have a more exciting example that I want to bring to you, but everything that Neville described about the rise of his family's fortune matches business records and reportage in West Indian newspapers.

Neville lived in Greenwich Village for many years. In the 1940s he was at 32 Washington Square on the west side of Washington Square Park. He spent many years happily there. Now, here was a story that interested me in his lectures and I determined to track down the truth of it. Neville was drafted into the Army on November 12, 1942, just a little less than a year into America's entry to

World War II, so it was at the height of war. Everybody was being drafted. He was a little old to be drafted. He was 37 at that time, but you could still be drafted up to age 45. He tells this story in several of his lectures.

He didn't want to be in the Army. He wanted no part of the war. He wanted to return home to Greenwich Village. At that time, he was married. He had a small daughter, Victoria or Vicky. He had a son from an earlier marriage. He wanted to go back to lecturing. He was in basic training in Louisiana. He asked his commanding officer for a discharge and the commanding officer definitively refused.

So Neville said that every night he would lay down in his cot and imagine himself back home in Greenwich Village, walking around Washington Square Park, back with his wife and family. Every night he'd go to bed in this sensation.

Night after night, he did this for several weeks. And he said that finally, out of the clear blue, the commanding officer came to him and said, "Do you still want to be discharged?" Neville said, "Yes, I do." "You're being honorably discharged," the officer told him.

As I read this, I doubted it. Why would the United States want to discharge a perfectly healthy, athletic male at the height of the America's entry into the Second World War? It made no sense. I started looking for Neville's military records to see if there were other things that would back this up. Neville claimed that he entered the military in late 1942 and then he was honorably discharged about four months later using nothing other than these mental-emotive techniques.

I found Neville's surviving military records. He was, in fact, inducted into the Army on November 12, 1942. I spoke to an Army public affairs spokesman who confirmed that Neville was honorably discharged in March 1943, which is the final record of his U.S. Army pay statement. The reason for the discharge in military records is that he had to return to a "vital civilian occupation." I said to the spokesman, "This man was a metaphysical lecturer, that is not seen as a vital civilian occupation." And he said to me, "Well, unfortunately, the rest of Mr. Goddard's records were destroyed in a fire at a military records facility 1973"—one year following Neville's death.

I know that Neville was back in New York City because *The New Yorker* magazine ran surprisingly extensive profile of him in September of 1943, which places him back on the circuit. He was depicted speaking all around town—in midtown in the Actor's Church, in Greenwich Village, and he completely resumed his career, this "vital civilian occupation" as a metaphysical lecturer. Now, I can't tell you what happened. I can only tell you that the forensics as he described them were accurate. This was one of several instances in which he describes an unlikely story, claims that he used his method as I've described it them you, and, while I can't tell you exactly what happened, I can tell you that the forensics line up.

Neville filled out an application for naturalization and citizenship on September 1, 1943. His address was 32 Washington Square at the time, his age 38 years old. Everything he described in terms of his whereabouts added up.

The Source

I want to say a quick word about where this philosophy came from. Where did Neville get these ideas? His thought was wholly original but everyone has antecedents of some kind. Neville was part of a movement that I call "the positive-thinking movement." Positive-mind metaphysics was a very American philosophy, and it was very much a homegrown philosophy, but, at the same time, every thought that's ever been thought has been encountered by sensitive people in the search extending back to the mythical Hermes, who ancient people in West and Near East considered the progenitor of all ideas and all intellect.

Hermetic philosophy was a Greek-Egyptian philosophy that was written about and set down in the Greek language in the city of Alexandria a few decades following the death of Christ. Neville quotes from one of the Hermetic books in the lecture "Inner Conversations." A central Hermetic theme is that through proper preparation, diet, meditation, and prayer, the individual can be permeated by divine forces. This was a key tenet of Hermeticism. This outlook was reborn during the Renaissance when scholars and translators came to venerate the figure of Hermes Trismegistus, or thrice-greatest Hermes, a Greek term of veneration of Egypt's god of intellect Thoth. Hermes Trismegistus, a mythical man-god, was considered a great figure of antiquity by Renaissance thinkers, of a vintage as old as Moses or Abraham or older still.

Renaissance translators initially believed that the Hermetic literature—tracts that were signed by Hermes Trismegistus, whose name was adopted by Greek-Egyptian scribes—extended back to primeval antiquity. Hermetic writings were considered the source of earliest wisdom. This literature was later correctly dated to late antiquity. After the re-dating, Hermetic ideas eventually fell out of vogue. Some of the intellectual lights of the Renaissance had placed great hopes that the writings attributed to Hermes Trismegistus possessed great antiquity. And when those hopes of antiquity were and these writings were accurately dated to late antiquity, the readjustment of the timeline, I think tragically for Western civilization, convinced many people that the whole project of the Hermetic literature was somehow compromised. For that reason there are, to this day, relatively few quality translations of the Hermetic literature. The dating issue assumed too great a proportion in people's minds. The fact is, all ancient literature, just like all religions, are built from earlier ideas, and I believe the Hermetic philosophy was a retention of much older oral philosophy. Most scholars today agree with that.

In any case, the Hermetic ideas faded. Including the core principle that the human form could be permeated by something higher and could itself attain a kind of creative and clairvoyant power. These ideas that were so arousing, that created such hope and intrigue during Renaissance, got pushed to the margins. But they eventually reentered the public mind in part through the influence of Franz Anton Mesmer (1734–1815), who was a lawyer and a self-styled physician of Viennese descent. Mesmer appeared in Paris in 1778, in the decade preceding the French Revolution. He entered into royal courts with this radical theory that all of life was animated by this invisible etheric fluid which he called *animal magnetism.*

Mesmer maintained that if you place an individual into a kind of trance state, what we would call a hypnotic trance—recall Neville talking about this state of drowsiness, this hypnagogic state—you could then realign his or her animal magnetism, this ethereal life fluid, and cure physical or mental diseases, and, according to practitioners, introduce powers such as clairvoyance or the ability to speak in unknown foreign tongues. You could heal. You could empower. You could get at the life stuff of the individual. I was recently in a Walgreen's drugstore and saw an ad reading, "Mysterious and Mesmerizing," for a skin lotion. It's funny how occult language, unmoored from its meaning, lingers in daily life.

Mesmer was feted in royal courts but his philosophy aroused suspicion. At the instigation of King Louis XVI, Mesmerism was discredited by a royal commission in 1784. This investigatory commission was chaired by Benjamin Franklin, who at the time was America's ambassador to France. The commission concluded that there was no such thing as animal magnetism and that whatever cures or effects were experienced under the influence of a mesmeric trance were "in the imagination." But there the committee left dangling its most extraordinary question. If it's "in the imagination," why should there be any effects at all?

Mesmer's greatest students edged away from the idea of animal magnetism as some physical, ethereal fluid. They believed something else was at work. In their struggle for answers, they arrived at the first descriptions of what we would later call subliminal mind and then the subconscious or unconscious mind. Mesmer's proteges did not possess a psychological vocabulary—they preceded and in some regards prefigured modern psychology—but they knew that *something* was evident and effective in his theory of animal magnetism. The best students morphed the master's theories into an early, rough iteration of the subconscious mind. This is an overlooked and crucial basis for the growth of modern psychology. The terms subliminal and subconscious mind began to be heard in the 1890s.

Mesmer died in 1815. But his ideas were taken up in many quarters including, fatefully, by a New England clockmaker named Phineas Quimby (1802–1866). Starting in the late 1830s, Quimby began to experiment with how states of *personal excitement* could make him feel better physically. Quimby suffered from tuberculosis and he discovered that when he would take vigorous carriage rides in the Maine countryside, the effects of tuberculosis would lift. Quimby began to probe the state of his mood and the state of his physical wellbeing. He treated others and became known as a mental healer in the mid-1840s.

At first, Quimby worked with a teenaged boy named Lucius Burkmar. Lucius would enter a trance or hypnagogic state from which he was said to be able to clairvoyantly view people's bodily organs and diagnose and prescribe cures for diseases. Quimby discovered that sometimes the cures that Lucius prescribed, which were often botanical remedies or herbal teas, had previously been prescribed by physicians—and did not work. But when Lucius prescribed them, *they often did work*. The difference, Quimby concluded, was in the *confidence of the patient*. Quimby stopped working with Lucius and encouraged patients to arouse mental energies on their own.

American medicine in the mid-1840s was in a horrendously underdeveloped state. It was the one area of the sciences in which American lagged behind Europe. People had some reason to be driven to mental healers and prayer healers because, if anything, they were less dangerous than most of what was then standard allopathic medicine, which involved measures that were medieval. Physicians were performing bloodletting, administering mercury and other poisons and narcotics. At the very least, the mental healing movement caused no harm.

And, according to historical letters, articles, and diaries, sometimes it did a lot of good. Someone who briefly served as a student to Quimby was Mary Baker Eddy (1821–1910), who founded her own movement called Christian Science. Eddy taught that the healing ministry of Christ is an ever-present fact that is still going on on Earth, and that individuals could be healed by the realization that there is only one true reality and that is this great divine mind that created the universe and that animates everything around us; and further that matter, these forms that we live in, and the floorboards underneath our feet, are not real. They are illusory, as are illness, prejudice, violence, and all human corruption. Eddy taught that through prayer and proper understanding of Scripture, the individual could be healed. She was a remarkable figure. Sometimes people will say, in a far too hasty way, "Well, she took all her ideas from Quimby." It's not that simple. Her interlude with Quimby in the early 1860s was vitally important in her development; but her ideas were uniquely her own. She was an extraordinary figure. I don't think we've taken full measure in this culture of how influential Mary Baker Eddy's ideas have been.

Another figure who become indirectly influential in this healing movement was Emanuel Swedenborg (1688–1772), a Swedish scientist and mystic who worked primarily in the 1700s. Swedenborg's central idea was that the mind is a conduit, a capillary, of cosmic laws, and everything that occurs in the world, including our own thoughts, mirrors events in an invisible world, a spiritual world, which we do not see but always interact with. Everything that men and women do on Earth, Swedenborg taught, is a reflection of something occurring in this unseen world, and our minds are almost like receiving stations, spiritual telegraphs, for messages and ideas from a cosmic plane in which we cannot directly participate but are vitally linked.

Swedenborg was an influence on a Methodist minister named Warren Felt Evans, who was also a contemporary of Quimby's, and who briefly worked with him. Evans wrote a book in 1869 called *The Mental Cure* which was the first book to use the term "new age" in the spiritual sense that it's used today. Evans believed that through prayer, proper direction of thought, use of affirmations, and assumption of a confident mental state, the individual could be cured. *The Mental Cure* is not read anywhere today. Yet it is a surprisingly sprightly book. You'd be surprised. When I first had to read *The Mental Cure* I braced myself but I found that its pages turn quite effortlessly. Evans was a brilliant writer. All of his books are obscure today. But he was a seminal figure in the creation of a positive-thinking movement.

More indirectly, the British poet William Blake also had a certain influence on this movement, and on Neville in particular. Blake believed that humans dwell in this coarse world where we are imprisoned in a fortress of illusions; but the one true mind, the great creative imagination of God, can course through us. We can "cleanse the doors of perception." We can feel the coursing of this great mind within us.

These are some of the same ideas that resounded in Hermeticism. There wasn't a direct connection, necessarily. First of all, there weren't many translations of some of the Hermetic literature, which a man like Blake could likely draw upon. People from different epochs and eras often arrived at these parallel cosmic ideas themselves. When academic writers approach New Thought or the positive-thinking movement, they sometimes make the mistake of conflating it with the idealist philosophy of figures like Berkeley, Kant, Hegel, and later Schopenhauer and Nietzsche. The positive-thinking figures were not directly influenced by the idealists. Those figures and their phraseology are absent in early positive-mind writings. People sometimes make the mistake of not realizing that in a country like America, which was a very agricultural country throughout most of the 19th century, little of this material was directly available.

As an example, consider the Tao Te Ching. This great ancient Chinese work on ethics and philosophy wasn't even translated into English until 1838. In the mid-1840s, there existed four

English-language copies in all of the United States. One was in the library at Harvard, one was in Ralph Waldo Emerson's library which he lent out, and two were in private hands. It wasn't like somebody like Phineas Quimby, the New England clockmaker, who was experimenting with moods and the body, could locate Taoist or Hermetic philosophy, or could even read translations of Hegel. Literacy aside, many of these things weren't accessible. It's a mistake to conclude that because one system of thought mirrors another, that the preceding system is necessarily the birth mother of the later one. In the rural environs of America, many of the positive-mind theorists were independently coming up with these ideas.

Moving into the 20th century, we encounter a figure who directly influenced Neville—French mind theorist Emile Coué (1857–1926). Coué was a largely self-trained hypnotherapist. He died in 1926, but shortly before he died, he made two lecture tours of the United States. Coué was hugely popular in the US and in England. He had a key theory, which rested on the principle that when you enter a sleepy drowsy state, the hypnagogic state, your mind is uniquely supple, suggestible, and powerful. Coué came up with a method to use in conjunction with this state. His system was so simple that critics mocked it. You've probably heard of it. Coué told people to gently repeat the mantra, "Day by day, in every way, I am getting better and better." He said you should lay in bed and recite this just as you're drifting off at night and again just as you're coming to in the morning. Whisper it twenty times to yourself. You could knot a piece of string twenty times and take that piece of string with you, keep it at your bedside, so you could count off your repetitions like a rosary.

Coué had many thousands of followers, but he also became a figure of ridicule because the critics said: "How could such a simple idea possibly do anything for anyone?" Of course, they would not try it. To their minds, it was prima facie nonsense. Such an attitude reminds me of the character of Dr. Zaius from *Planet of the Apes* insisting that flight is a physical impossibility. Thought in the absence of experience is the impoverishment of our intellectual culture. Certainty in the absence of personal experience precludes effort.

In addition to the uses of hypnagogia, another of Coué's ideas appeared in Neville's thought system. You can find the language from time to time in Neville's lectures and writing. That is, within human beings exist two forces: *will* and *imagination*. The *will* is intellectual self-determination. The *imagination* is the mental images and emotionally conditioned reactions that populate our psyches, particularly with regard to self-image. Coué said that when imagination and will are in conflict, *imagination always win*. Your emotional state always overcomes your intellect.

As an example, Coué said, place a wooden plank on the floor and ask an average person to walk across it. He or she will have no problem. But if you raise that same wooden plank twenty feet off the ground, in many cases the person will be petrified even though there's no difference in the physical demand. They are capable of walking across it. The risk of falling is minimal. *The change in condition alone creates an emotional state that makes them more nervous and hence accident prone.* Coué believed it necessary to cultivate new imaginative images of ourselves. We cannot do that through the intellect alone. But we can do so by making using of this very subtle hypnagogic state. He called his method auto-suggestion. It was self-hypnosis essentially. Neville adopted the method, if not the same assumptions behind it.

The Mystic in Life

There are few pictures of Neville. His smiles glowingly in rare pictures toward the end of his life. He died young at age 67 in 1972. He died of heart failure in West Hollywood where he was living with his family. Until the end, his voice and his powers of communication never left him. They absolutely resonated.

It's interesting sometimes to look at the lives of mystical figures like Neville who are hard to pin down, but who did lead domestic lives. There was a little piece in the *Los Angeles Times* on October 21, 1962: "Ms. Goddard Named as College President." It went on, "Miss Victoria Goddard, daughter of Mr. and Mrs. Neville Goddard, has been appointed co-chairman of campus publicity by the student government president at Russell Sage College for New York. She is an English major." This was Neville's daughter.

Now, Victoria Goddard or Vicky as she's known, is still living. She lives in Los Angeles in the family house that she once resided in with her parents. She avoids publicity and contact with people who are interested in Neville's ideas. I've tried to reach out to her but she has no interest in being in touch. She did give her approval indirectly to an anthology of Neville's writings that I wrote an introduction to, but she doesn't want contact with his students. She wants to lead her own existence. But it's funny sometimes we come across little things like this article or a photograph and realize that every one of us share the same workaday concerns.

For all of Neville's wonderful mystical theories, I just have to share this little discourse that he went into about Liquid-Plumr in a lecture that he delivered in 1970. I found this a delightful reminder of how the ordinary steps into all of our lives even when we're trying to deal with cosmic and mystical concerns. He told an audience in 1970:

So you buy something because of highly publicized TV promotions. Someone highly publicized what is called "Liquid-Plumr." And so I had some moment in my bathroom where the sink was all stopped up, so I got the Liquid-Plumr. Poured it in, in abundance. It said it's heavier than water, and it would go all the way down and just eat up everything that is organic and will not hurt anything that is not organic, so I poured it in. Water still remained; it didn't go down. Called the plumber the next day. He couldn't come that day but he would come the next day. So it was forty-eight hours. So when he came the entire sink was eaten away by the Liquid-Plumr. So I asked him: "Does this thing work?" He said: "It does for two people: the one who manufactures it, and the one who sells it." They are the only ones who profit by the Liquid-Plumr. And so you turned on the TV and you saw it and you bought it. It is still on TV and I am sinning, because to sin by silence when I should protest makes cowards of us all. But I haven't protested to the station that advertises this nonsense and I haven't protested to the place where I got it or to anyone who manufactures it, so I am the silent sinner. Multiply me because of my embarrassment. Here is a sink completely eaten up by Liquid-Plumr.

"The silent sinner," he called himself. I lodge letters of protest and phone calls from time to time, so I can sympathize with everything Neville says here.

Neville published a variety of books during his lifetime, most of them quite short. There was a company in Los Angeles called G and J Publishing which issued most of his books. A symbol appeared on most of his covers, which he devised himself. It was a heart with an eye to symbolize eternal vision, inner vision, and it was part of a fruit-bearing tree. As the emotive state of man conceives, so the tree brings forth fruit.

In 1964, Neville published an extremely rare pamphlet called, *He Breaks The Shell*. On its cover you can see a little cherub or angelic figure coming out of a human head. Neville described this mystical experience and said that this is an experience that all of us will have either in this lifetime or another; and that the whole purpose of human existence is to be reborn from your imagination; and your imagination, as we experience it, is physically lodged in your skull, entombed in this kind of a womb. Christ was crucified in Golgotha, place of the skull. Neville believed that we each will be reborn from within our own skull, and that we will have an actual physical experience, maybe in the form of a dream, but a vivid, tactile experience of being reborn from out of the base of our skull. We will know, in that moment, that we are fulfilling our essential purpose.

He described this quite vividly. He had this experience in New York City in 1959 where he had an enormously tactile, sensationally real dream of being reborn from out of the skull. Minerva was said to have been reborn from the skull of Zeus or Jupiter. Christ was crucified at the place of the skull. "You and I," Neville said, "will be reborn from within our skull." In the late 1960s a booking agent told him, "Listen, you've got to stop telling this story at your talks. It's freaking everyone out. People want to hear the get-rich stuff." He told Neville that he if did not change course he'd have no audience left. "Then I'll tell it to the bare walls," Neville replied. He spoke of his mystical experience for the rest of his career until he died in 1972.

I reissued one of Neville's books recently, *The Power of Awareness*. I felt that, for the first time, Neville's books needed to be packaged in a way that fits their dignity, and this is a beautiful edition that I took great joy in working on because I thought it represented him with the right degree of dignity.

I want to quote from Neville's voice. He spoke in such beautiful, resonant language, so unhaltingly, never a pause, never an uncertainty. He knew his outlook so well, he could share it effortlessly. Here is his voice.

So I'm telling you of the power within you and that power is your own wonderful human imagination. And that is the only God in the world. There is no other God. That is the Jesus Christ of Scripture, so tonight take it seriously. If you really have an objective in this world and you're waiting for something to happen on the outside to make it so, forget it. Do it in your own wonderful human imagination. Actually bring it into being in your own imagination. Conjure a scene which would imply the fulfillment of that dream and lose yourself in the action as you contemplate it, and completely lose yourself in that state. If you're completely absorbed in it, you will objectify it and you will see it seemingly independent of your perception of it. But even if you do not have that intensity, if you lose yourself in it and feel it to true—the imaginal act—then drop it. In a way you do not know, it will become true.

If you are interested in hearing more of Neville, you can go online and find lectures that are posted on YouTube and almost everywhere. He allowed people who came to presentations to tape record them and freely distribute them. He claimed copyright over nothing, and that, to me, is the mark of a real leader. That's the mark of a real thinker. You don't have to join anything. You don't have to ask anybody permission for anything. You don't have to pay any dues. You don't have to buy anything. You just start.

Neville's Circle

I want to say a quick word about some of the people who have been influenced by Neville today. One of them is the major-league baseball pitcher, Barry Zito, who actually introduced me to Neville. I was doing an article about Barry in 2003 and he said to me, "Oh, you must be into Neville," and I said, "I've never heard of him." He said, "Really? You never heard of him?" He was the first one who got me interested in Neville's thought, and that was a huge influence in my life. It was almost 10 years ago to this very day and in many regards put me where I am today.

The New Age writer Wayne Dyer wrote a lot about Neville in his most recent book which is called *Wishes Fulfilled*. But a really remarkable influence that Neville brought into the world came in the form his subtle impact on the writer, Carlos Castaneda, of whom I'm a great admirer. I want to read a short passage from my forthcoming book, *One Simple Idea*:

> By the mid-1950s, Neville's life story exerted a powerful pull on a budding writer whose own memoirs of mystic discovery later made him a near-household name: Carlos Castaneda. Castaneda told his own tales of tutelage under a mysterious instructor, in his case a Native American

sorcerer named Don Juan. Castaneda first discovered Neville through an early love interest in Los Angeles, Margaret Runyan, who was among Neville's most dedicated students. A cousin of American storyteller Damon Runyon, Margaret wooed the stocky Latin art student at a friend's house, slipping Carlos a slender Neville volume called *The Search,* in which she had inscribed her name and phone number. The two became lovers and later husband and wife. Runyan spoke frequently to Castaneda about her mystical teacher Neville, but he responded with little more than mild interest—with one exception.

In her memoirs, Runyan recalled Castaneda growing fascinated when the conversation turned to Neville's discipleship under an exotic teacher. She wrote:

It was more than the message that attracted Carlos, it was Neville himself. He was so mysterious. Nobody was really sure who he was or where he had come from. There were vague references to Barbados in the West Indies and his being the son of an ultra-rich plantation family, but nobody knew for sure. They couldn't even be sure about this Abdullah business, his Indian teacher, who was always way back there in the jungle, or someplace. The only thing you really knew was that Neville was here and that he might be back next week, but then again . . .

"There was," Runyon concluded, "a certain power in that position, an appealing kind of freedom in the lack of past and Carlos knew it."

Carlos knew it. Both Neville and Castaneda were dealing the same basic idea, and one that has a certain pedigree in America's alternative spiritual culture: tutelage under hidden spiritual masters.

Neville again and again told this story, that there was a turbaned black man of Jewish descent who tutored him starting in 1931 in kabbalah, Scripture, number symbolism, and mental metaphysics. He described Abdullah as this somewhat taciturn, mysterious figure who he met one day at a metaphysical lecture in 1931. Neville walked in and Abdullah said to him, "Neville, you're six months late." Neville said, "I had never seen this man before." Abdullah continued, "The brothers told me you were coming and you're six months late." He said they spent the next five years together studying.

Neville had his first true awakening experience in the winter of 1933. He was dying to get out of the Manhattan winter. He wanted to spend Christmas back home with his family in Barbados. He had no money and Abdullah said to him, "Walk the streets of Manhattan as if you are there and you shall be." And so Neville said he would walk the gray wintry streets of the Upper West Side with the feeling that he was in the palm-lined lanes of Barbados. He would go to see Abdullah, telling him, "It isn't working. I'm still here." And Abdullah would slam the door in his face and say, "You're not here. You're in Barbados."

Then one day, before the last ship departed for Barbados, his brother, Victor, from out of the blue, without any physical intercession on Neville's part, sent him a first-class steamer ticket and $50. "Come spend winter with us in Barbados," he wrote. Neville said he was transformed by the experience. He felt that it was Abdullah's law of mental assumption came to his rescue.

Now, this idea of mysterious spiritual masters got popularized in modern Western culture through the influence of Madame Blavatsky and her partner Colonel Henry Steel Olcott who founded the movement of Theosophy in New York City in 1975. They claimed to be under the tutelage of hidden spiritual masters, Master Koot Hoomi, who was said to be Tibetan, and Master Morya who was said to be Indian. These adepts, they said, would send them phenomenally produced letters, advising them what to do, giving them directions, giving them advice, giving them succor. Around that time, Colonel Olcott and Madame Blavatsky were living in a building which is still standing at the corner of 8th Avenue of West 47th Street which was known as the Lamasery, their headquarters or salon, where they dwelt on the second floor. Today it is an Econo Lodge. None of the people who worked there were very entranced with my attempts to explain the history of the building.

Colonel Olcott said that one time in the winter of 1877, Master Morya materialized in his room and directed him and Madame Blavatsky to relocate to the nation of India, which they did the following year. They helped instigate the Indian independence movement. Olcott went on speaking tours all over the Near East, Far

East, Japan, Sri Lanka. He helped instigate a rebirth of Buddhism throughout the East. Blavatsky and Olcott were enormously effective in their way. Colonel Olcott attributed all of it to the presence of these mysterious spiritual masters, these great turbaned figures somewhere from the East who had given them instruction.

Now, I first wrote about Neville in an article that was published in February 2005 in *Science of Mind* magazine called "Searching for Neville Goddard." Things had been fairly quiet around Neville for many years, and that article attracted a lot of interest. I started receiving phone calls and e-mail after e-mail asking me, who was Abdullah? Did he exist? Could he be identified? I would tell people at the time that I thought Abdullah was a kind of a mythos that Neville might have borrowed, clipped and pasted, from Theosophy. I didn't think there was any evidence to show that Abdullah was a real person, and I thought the dramatic claims around him were probably Neville's mythmaking.

Now, to my surprise, I discovered something about Abdullah through another figure in the positive thinking movement, a man named Joseph Murphy, who died in 1981, and who wrote a very popular book, which some of you may have read, called *The Power of Your Subconscious Mind*. Shortly before his death, Murphy gave a series of interviews to a French-speaking minister from Quebec. The interviewer published his book only in French with Quebec press. It is called *Dialogues with Joseph Murphy* and in these interviews Murphy offhandedly remarks that he, too, was a student of Abdullah. Murphy actually came to New York around the same time as Neville in 1922. He migrated from Ireland. Murphy worked as a pharmacist at the Algonquin Hotel. They used to have a little pharmacy in their lobby. And Murphy also became a metaphysical lecturer and was acquainted with Neville for several years. He stated very simply and matter-of-factly that Abdullah was his teacher too, and that he was a very real man.

I began to look around and correspond with people, and I came to feel, over the past few years, that I happened upon a figure who might actually be Abdullah. He was Arnold Josiah Ford. Ford was a mystic, black nationalist, and part of a movement called the Black Hebrew Movement which still exists in various forms. Ford was born in Barbados, Neville's home island, in 1877. Ford emigrated to Harlem in 1910. He became involved with Marcus Garvey's Universal Negro Improvement Association, of which he was musical director. In surviving photographs Ford, like Abdullah, is turbaned.

In addition to being a dedicated follower of Marcus Garvey—who had his own mind-power metaphysics, about which I'll say a quick word in a moment—Ford was also part of a movement called Ethiopianism. It was a precursor to Rastafarianism. Ford believed, as the Rastafarian people do, as many other people do with good reason, that Ethiopia, one of the oldest continuous civilizations on Earth and one of the most populous nations in Africa, was home to a lost tribe of Israel, which, in this line of teaching, had its own blend of what we know as traditional historical Judaism and mystical teachings and mental metaphysics.

The movement of Ethiopianism believed that this lost African-Israelite tribe harbored a great wealth of ancient teachings that had been lost to most modern people. The Ethiopianism movement believed in mind-power metaphysics and mental healing. Ford was considered a rabbi and he had his own African-American congregation in Harlem. He described himself a man of authentic Israelite and Jewish descent. Writing in 1946, occult philosopher Israel Regardie described Neville's Abdullah as an "Ethiopian rabbi." Regardie, who had been a secretary to the occultist, Aleister Crowley, is quoted on Neville in the introduction.

According to census records, Ford was living in Harlem 1931. He identified his occupation to the census taker as rabbi. That was the same year that Neville met Abdullah. (Although he later gave Abdullah's address as the Upper West Side, not Harlem.) Neville may have been playing around with the name a little bit. He would affectionately refer to Abdullah in his lectures as *Ab*. Ab is a variant of the Hebrew word *abba* for father. Perhaps he saw Abdullah, Ford, as kind of a father figure. He said they studied metaphysics, Scripture, Kabbalah together for five years. Ford has been written about in histories of the Black Hebrew Movement as a key figure who brought authentic knowledge of the Hebrew language, Talmud, and Kabbalah into the Black Hebrew Movement as it existed in Harlem at that time.

Ford was a person of some learning. He was, as I said, a follower of Marcus Garvey, a figure about whom I write in *Occult America*. Garvey has not been properly understood in our culture. He was a pioneering black nationalist figure. He was a great pioneering activist and voice of liberation. He was also very much into his own brand of mental metaphysics. You might recognize this statement of Garvey's which Bob Marley adapted in the lyrics to *Redemption Song:* "We are going to emancipate ourselves from mental slavery because whilst others might free the body, none but ourselves can free the mind." Garvey's speeches are shot through with New Thought language, with the language of mental metaphysics. This was an essential part of Garvey's outlook. This perspective was also essential to the culture of Ethiopianism, which saw Ethiopia's crowned emperor, Haile Selassie, who was coronated in 1930, as a messianic figure. The movement of Ethiopianism morphed into Rastafarianism. It started in the mid-1930s.

Now, there are a lot of correspondences between Arnold Josiah Ford and Neville's description of Abdullah, including physical correspondences, the turban and such. But for all that I've noted, the timeline does not match up sufficiently to make any of this conclusive; because Ford left America sometime in 1931, and he moved to the Ethiopian countryside. After Haile Selassie was coronated as emperor, he offered a land grant to any African-American willing to emigrate to Ethiopia. The emperor saw Ethiopia in a way that matched Ford's ideals as a kind of African-Israel. Haile Selassie wanted Afro-Caribbean and Afro-American people to move, or to come home as he saw it, to Ethiopia, so he offered land grants.

Ford and about thirty followers of Ethiopianism in New York accepted the land grants. There's been some debate about when Ford left, but I have a *New York Times* article that places Ford in New York City still in December 1930. He didn't leave until 1931. That was the same year that Neville said they met. The timeline doesn't match up because Neville said they studied together for five years, so it's possible that Ford was one of several teachers that Neville had, and he created a kind of composite figure who he called Abdullah, Ab, father, of whom Ford may have been a part.

Now, in a coda to Ford's life, I must take note that it was a tougher and braver and more brutal existence back then in some regards. Ford, who for 20 years has been living as a musician and a rabbi in Harlem, moved to rural Ethiopia, the northern part of this nation, to accept Haile Selassie's land grant. He died there in 1935. Tragically, there are no records of Ford's life in Ethiopia. It must have been very difficult. Imagine being a metropolitan person and uprooting yourself to a completely rural setting in a developing nation in the 1930s, and Mussolini is beating the war drum, and Mussolini's fascist troops invaded Ethiopia just weeks after Ford's death, across the north border. This was a man who put himself through tremendous ordeals for his principles. I cannot conclude that Ford was Abdullah. But Murphy's testimony suggests that there *was* an Abdullah, and I think Ford corresponds in many ways—and I write about this in *One Simple Idea*; there probably is some intersection there.

There's another figure I want to mention of a very different kind whose thought had some indirect intersection with Neville's, and that is Aleister Crowley, the British occultist. Crowley made a very interesting statement in a book that he received in a way that we might call channeled perception in 1904; it was later published broadly in 1938 called *The Book of the Law*. In his introduction, Crowley writes:

Each of us has thus an universe of his own, but it is the same universe for each one as soon as it includes all possible experience. This implies the extension of consciousness to include all other consciousnesses. In our present stage, the object that you see is never the same as the one that I see; we infer that it is the same because your experience tallies with mine on so many points that the actual differences of our observation are negligible . . . Yet all the time neither of us can know anything . . . at all beyond the total impression made on our respective minds.

Neville said something similar:

Do you realize that no two people live in the same world? We may be together now in this room, but we will go home tonight and close our doors on entirely different worlds. Tomorrow, we will go to work where we'll meet others but each one of us lives in our own mental and physical world.

Neville meant this in the most literal sense. He believed that every individual, possessed of his or her own imagination, is God, and that everyone you see, including me standing in this room, is rooted in you, as you are ultimately rooted in God.

You exist in this world of infinite possibilities and realities, and that, in fact, when you mentally picture something, you're not creating it—it already exists. You're claiming it. The very fact of being able to experience it mentally confirms that in this world of infinite possibilities, where imagination is the ultimate creative agent, everything that you can picture *already is*.

Mind Science

Some of the things that Neville said prefigured studies both in psychical research and quantum physics. I want to say a quick word about that. One of my heroes is, J.B. Rhine, a psychical researcher who performed tens of thousands of trials at Duke University in the 1930s and beyond to test for clairvoyant perception. Rhine often used a five-suit deck of cards called Zener cards; if you were guessing a card, you had a one-in-five chance, 20 percent, of naming the right card. As Rhine documented in literally tens of thousands of trials, with meticulous clinical control, certain individuals persistently, under controlled conditions, scored higher than a chance hit of 20 percent.

It wasn't always dramatically higher. It wasn't like Zeus was aiming lightning bolts at the Earth. But if someone over the course of thousands of trials keeps scoring 25 percent, 26 percent, 27 percent, beyond all chance possibility, and the results are parsed, juried, gone over, reviewed, you have some anomalous transfer of information going on in a laboratory setting. Rhine's research was real. And Rhine noticed—and he had this quietly monumental way of describing things, he would make some observation in a footnote that could be extraordinary—that the correlation to a high success rate of hits on the Zener cards was usually a feeling of enthusiasm, positive expectation, hopefulness, belief in the possibility of ESP, and an encouraging environment. Then when boredom or physical exhaustion would set in, or interest would wane, the results would go down. If interest was somehow renewed, revised, if there was a feeling of comity in the testing room, the results would go up.

We as a culture haven't begun to deal with the implications of Rhine's experiments. There was another parapsychologist, Charles Honorton, who began a series of experiments in 1970s—I see him as Rhine's successor—called the *ganzfeld* experiments. Ganzfeld is German for whole field. Honorton experimented on subjects who were in a hypnagogic state, the state of drowsiness. Honorton and his collaborators theorized that if you could induce the near-sleep state in an individual, put somebody in conditions of comfortable isolation, fit them with eye coverings and headphones emitting white noise or some kind of negative sound to listen to, put them in a greatly relaxed state, it might be possible to heighten the appearance of some kind of clairvoyant faculty.

His test was to place a subject, a receiver, into a comfortable isolation tank, and to place another subject, a sender, in a different room. Then the sender attempted to mentally convey an image—such as a flower, a rocket, a boat, or something else—to the receiver, and see what happens. These tests generally used four images. Three were decoys, one was actual. Again, in certain subjects, and also in the subjects as a whole in the form of meta-analysis, Honorton found over and over again results that showed a higher than 25 percent chance hit when subjects were placed into the hypnagogic state.

We're in this state all the time. When you're napping, when you're dozing off at your desk, when you're going to sleep at night, when you're waking up in the morning. Neville's message is: *use it.* Honorton died very young in 1992 at age 46. He had suffered health problems his whole life. If he had lived, his name would, I believe, be as well-known as J.B. Rhine. He was a great parapsychologist.

There's another field burgeoning today called neuroplasticity that relates to some of Neville's sights. In short, brain imaging shows that repeat thoughts change the pathways through which electrical impulses travel in your brain. This has been used to treat obsessive compulsive disorder. A research psychologist named Jeffery Schwartz at UCLA has devised a program that ameliorates and dissipates obsessive thoughts. Schwartz's program teaches patients and people in his clinical trials to substitute something in place of an obsessive thought at the very moment they experience it. This diversion may be a pleasurable physical activity, listening to music, jogging, whatever they want, just anything that gets them off that obsessive thought. Schwartz has found through brain imaging, and many scientists have replicated this data, that if you repeat an exercise like that, eventually biologic changes manifest in the brain, neuropathways change, thoughts themselves alter brain biology as far as electrical impulses are concerned.

A New Thought writer in 1911, who theorized without any of the contemporary brain imaging and neuroscience, came up with exactly the same prescription. His name was John Henry Randall. Randall called it *substitution.* His language and the language used today by 21st century researchers in neuroplasticity is extraordinarily similar.

Finally, we have emerging from the field of quantum physics an extraordinary set of questions, which have been coming at us actually for 80-plus years, about the extent to which observation influences the manifestation of subatomic particles. I want to give a very brief example. Basically, quantum physics experiments have shown that if you direct a wave of particles, often in the form of a light wave, at a target system, perhaps a double-slit box or two boxes, the wave of light will collapse into a particle state, it will go from a wave state to a particle state. This occurs when a conscious observer is present or a measurement is occurring. Interference patterns demonstrate that the particle-like properties of wave of light *at one time appeared in both boxes*. Only when someone decided to look or to take a measurement did the particles become localized in one box.

In 1935, physicist Erwin Schrodinger noted that the conclusions of these quantum experiments were so outrageous, were so contrary to all observed experience, that he devised a thought experiment called Schrodinger's Cat in order to highlight this surreality. Schrodinger did not intend his thought experiment to endorse quantum theorizing. He intended it to compel quantum theorists to deal with the ultimate and, what he considered, absurdist conclusions of their theories—theories which have never been overturned, theories which have been affirmed for 80 years. Now, Schrodinger's Cat comes down to this, it can be put this way: You take two boxes. You put a cat into one of the two boxes. You direct a subatomic particle at the boxes. One box is empty, one box holds the cat. Inside the box with the cat is what he called a "diabolical device." This diabolical device trips a beaker of poison when it comes in contact with a subatomic particle, thus killing the cat.

So, you do your experiment. You direct the particle and you go to check the boxes. Which box is the particle in? Is the cat dead? Is the cat alive? The cat is *both*, Schrodinger insisted. It must be *both* because the subatomic particle can be shown to exist in more than one place, in a wave state, until someone checks, and thus localizes it into a particle state, occupying one place. Hence, you must allow for both outcomes—you have a dead/alive cat. That makes no sense. All of lived experience says that you've got two boxes; you've got one cat; the cat's dead if you fired into the box with the cat; or the cat's alive if you fired into the other box. Schrodinger said, "Not so." Interference experiments demonstrate that at one point the subatomic particle was in a *wave state*; it was non-local; it existed only in potential; it existed in both boxes and, given the nature of quantum observation, potentially everywhere. It is only when you go to check and open one of the boxes that the particle becomes localized. *It was in both boxes until a conscious observer made the decision to check.*

A later group of physicists argued there's no doubting Schrodinger's conclusion, and in fact, if you were to check eight hours later, you would not only find a cat that was living/dead, but you would find a living cat that was hungry because it hadn't been fed for eight hours. The timing itself created a past, present, and future for the cat—a reality selected out of infinite possibilities. Schrodinger didn't intend for his thought experiment to affirm this radical departure from reality. He intended it to expose what he considered the absurdist conclusions of quantum physics. But quantum physics data kept mounting and mounting, and Schrodinger's thought experiment became to some physicists a very real illustration of the extraordinary physical impossibilities that we were seeing in the world of quantum physics.

The implication is that we live in a serial universe—that there are infinite realities, whether we experience them or not; and our experience of one of these realties rests on observation. If we can extrapolate from the extraordinary behaviors of subatomic particles, it stands to reason that parallel events and potentials are all are occurring simultaneously. Why don't we experience any of this? Our world is seemingly controlled by Newtonian mechanics. There aren't dead/alive cats. There are singular events. Why don't we experience quantum reality?

Today, a theory that makes the rounds among quantum physicists that when something gets bigger and bigger—remember these experiments are done on subatomic particles, the smallest isolated fragments of matter—when we pull back from a microscopic view of things, we experience what is known as "information leakage." The world gets less and less clear as it gets bigger; as we exit the subatomic level and enter the mechanical level that is familiar, we lose information about what's really going on.

American philosopher William James made the same observation in 1902. James said that when you view an object under a microscope, you're getting so much information; but more and more of that information is lost as you pan back. This is true of all human experience. A cohort of quantum physicists today says the same thing: that the actions of the particle lab are occurring around us always, but we don't know it because we lose information in this coarse physical world that we live in.

Neville said something similar. He said that you radiate the world around you by the persuasiveness of your imagination and feelings. A quantum physicist might call this observation. But in our three-dimensional world, Neville said, time beats so slowly that we do not always observe the relationship between the visible world and our inner nature. You and I can contemplate a desire and become it, but because of the slowness of time, it is easy to forget what we formerly set out to worship or destroy. Quantum physicists speak of "information leakage;" Neville basically spoke of "time leakage." Time moves so slowly for us that we lose the sense of cause and effect.

"Scientists will one day explain why there is a serial universe," Neville said in 1948, "but in practice, how you use the serial universe to change the future is more important."

TRY

I want to leave you with a slogan of an American occultist P.B. Randolph who lived in New York City. He was a man of African-American descent and a tremendously original thinker and mystical experimenter. He died at the young age of 49 in 1875. This was his personal slogan: *TRY*. That's all. *TRY*. This slogan later appeared in letters signed by the spiritual masters Koot Hoomi and Morya, which started reaching Colonel Henry Steel Olcott in 1870s. The first appeared about two months before Randolph's death. The letters used the same slogan: *TRY*.

What you're hearing now is something to try. Neville's challenge was as ultimate as it was simple: "Put my ideas to the test." Prove them to yourself or dismiss them, but what a tragedy would be not to try. It's all so simple.

I want to conclude with words from William Blake, who was one of Neville's key inspirations later in life. Blake described the coarsened world of the senses that we live in. He described such things sometimes in matters of geography. When he would say England, he didn't mean England the nation exactly. He meant the coarse world in which men and women find themselves, the world in which we see so little, and the parameters close in so tightly that we don't know what's really going on. Then the poet would talk about Jerusalem, which he saw as a greater world, as a reality, created through the divine imagination, which runs through all men and women.

I want to close with William Blake's ode "Jerusalem" from 1810. I hope you'll try to hear these words as Neville himself heard them.

And did those feet in ancient time
Walk upon Englands mountains green:

And was the holy Lamb of God,
On Englands pleasant pastures seen!

And did the Countenance Divine,
Shine forth upon our clouded hills?
And was Jerusalem builded here,
Among these dark Satanic Mills?

Bring me my Bow of burning gold:
Bring me my arrows of desire:
Bring me my Spear: O clouds unfold!
Bring me my Chariot of fire!

I will not cease from Mental Fight,
Nor shall my sword sleep in my hand:
Till we have built Jerusalem,
In Englands green & pleasant Land.

Questions and Answers

If there are a few questions, I'd be happy to take them.

Speaker: Can you do multiple wishes, say if there are three that you wish?

Mitch: Neville's own students in his lifetime asked him that very thing, and I'm in the same place myself because it's hard sometimes to limit one's wishes to one thing. Neville felt it was more effective if you limit it to one thing at a time; but he said that this was by no means a limit, you didn't have to limit yourself. The key thing is to feel the desire intensely and to hold your mental emotive picture with clarity and simplicity, and to stick with it. He did say he felt that at the time interval would be lessened if you limit yourself to one thing at a time. That was his practice, but he did not call it a must.

Speaker: I wanted something that didn't last, so to try to achieve that, do I meditate on it? How do I get result?

Mitch: Neville's idea was to enact a scene that would naturally transpire when the desired thing comes to pass. There may be many events that would transpire if that thing came to pass, but he said to select just one that has a particular emotional resonance, and then see yourself doing it over and over. Something as simple as a handshake or climbing a ladder. Just take one that has act emotional gravity and be persistent.

Speaker: Do you think that given his predilection for inner vision that there's any evidence suggest that Abdullah may have been a channel? Abdullah may have been a channel or a channel within Neville?

Mitch: Oh, that's an interesting question. He always referred to Abdullah as a flesh-and-blood figure, and he said Abdullah lived in an apartment on West 72nd Street, which I've visited, and he would talk about Abdullah in very physical, vivid terms, so he certainly described him as a flesh-and-blood being.

Speaker: You described many of the techniques, including the technique of walking in a cold winter day to get the feeling of being in another place. This is just other technique for the astral body. Basically, what he's describing is the emotional astral body being developed, of which one expression would be manifesting that state here, but it sounds like he could easily develop another technique because this sounds very limited.

Mitch: He does represent techniques such as walking and imagining himself in the palm tree-lined lanes in Barbados; but he most often came back to this idea of physical immobility and the uses of a hypnagogic state, that drowsy state. He again and again said that others can experiment, and should experiment, but that he personally found that to be the simplest and the most effective method. He would say sometimes he would enter the hypnagogic state and just feel thankful or try to seize upon one expression like *it is wonderful*. He might do that if he didn't have a specific thing that he was longing for at that moment. So he did experiment with some other techniques and points of view. He did said one lecture, "You praise others and you will shine," because it was very important to try to use these techniques to the benefit of another person. For example, if you have a friend who's looking for a job, you might form the mental picture of congratulating him or her on finding the perfect job because Neville believed in the oneness of humanity in the absolute most literal sense. There was no sentimentality about it. He felt that every individual was God.

Speaker: Did he say that he believed that the universe is holographic?

Mitch: He would say, and again, he sometimes made statements more in passing than full on, but he would say explicitly that we live in a universe of infinite possibilities, and everything that you desire, by the very fact of desiring it, because your imagination is a creative agent, already exists. It is a question of just claiming it, which is why it's so important to think from the desire fulfilled. It doesn't matter if you open your eyes or your checkbook or anything else and, of course, reality as we presently know it comes rushing back in. You must continue to think from the wish fulfilled, which he said was tantamount to selecting a reality that already existed. Schrodinger said there's a dead/alive cat. Neville would have said there are infinite outcomes and they all exist.

Speaker: Regarding the slowness of time, I'm curious what his thoughts were as far as the timetables for his technique.

Mitch: He said that we experience definite time intervals and that a time interval is part of the nature of our existence. I may want a new house and I may want that house right now, and I may think from the end of having that house, but he said, in effect, "The fact of the world that we experience here and now is that the trees have to grow to produce wood. The wood has to be harvested and the carpenter has to cut it. There will be time intervals." And he would say, "Your time interval could be an hour, it could be a month, it could be weeks, it could be years." There is a time interval. You nonetheless must stick to the ideal and try to make it just exquisitely effortless. He didn't endorse using the will. This isn't about saying, "I'm going to think this way." It is going into this meditative or drowsy or hypnagogic state, picturing something that confirms the realization of your desire, and feeling it emotionally; he said that when the method fails maybe it's because you're trying too hard. Neville wanted people to understand that there is an exquisite ease that one should feel with exercises.

Speaker: It sounds like he's saying that an emphasis on pure will would upset that balance.

Mitch: Yes. He used the word receptivity and he used the term time interval.

Speaker: Did Neville ever include other ideas outside of his system?

Mitch: He made very few references to other thought systems. He would frequently quote Scripture, mostly the New Testament. He felt the New Testament was a great blueprint and metaphor for human development in the figure of Christ. He felt that the Old Testament was suggestive of the promise and the New Testament was fulfilling of the promise, and beyond that he made little reference to other thought systems. He was chiefly interested in Scripture. He would talk about numbers; he loved symbolism. In his book *Your Faith Is Your Fortune* he talked about certain aspects of the zodiac, astrology, and number symbolism; but as time passed, he made fewer references to other systems. Every now and again he'd use a piece of language where I'll detect Emile Coué echoed; but so much of what we talked about really came from his own description of the world through his own experience. He made little reference to other systems.

Speaker: I started reading your book *Occult America* and there was a question in my mind—you write that a lot of positive thinkers and people in New Age in American history have, on the one hand, kind of advocated basic techniques and methods for selfish success and money, and, on the other hand, a lot of the better writers in New Age and New Thought were passionately involved with and concerned about social movements. Where did Neville fall in that dichotomy?

Mitch: That's a wonderful question and that was an aspect for me that made it difficult to first enter Neville's work, because he had no social concerns in the conventional sense, and if people raised social concerns, he would push them aside and would insist that the world you see, whether it is of beauty or violence, is self-created. Prove the theory to yourself and then use the theory as you wish. You want to eliminate suffering? Eliminate suffering. But he ardently rejected fealty to any kind of social movement or ideal. He believed that coming into one's awareness of the godlike nature of imagination, of the literal God presence of the imagination, of having the experience of being reborn through one's skull, was the essential human task.

Speaker: As you said in your own book, a lot the 19th century Spiritualists were involved in movements like suffragism and abolitionism.

Mitch: Yes. Well, you know, these radical movements, radical political movements and radical spiritual movements, avant-garde politics, avant-garde spirituality, they all intersect. We often fail to understand how a figure like Marcus Garvey, for example, was involved with mental metaphysics; but as you get closer to the real lives of these people, the connection becomes more natural because they craved a new social order both spiritually and socially.

A Neville Goddard Timeline

1905: Neville Lancelot Goddard is born on February 19 to a British family in St. Michael, Barbados, the fourth child in a family of nine boys and one girl.

1922: At age seventeen Neville relocates to New York City to study theater. He makes a career as an actor and dancer on stage and silent screen, landing roles on Broadway, silent film, and touring Europe as part of a dance troupe.

1923: Neville briefly marries Mildred Mary Hughes, with whom he has a son, Joseph Goddard, born the following year.

1929: Neville marked this as the year that begin his mystical journey: "Early in the morning, maybe about three-thirty or four o'clock, I was taken in spirit into the Divine Council where the gods hold converse." (lecture from *Immortal Man*, 1977)

1931: After several years of occult study, Neville meets his teacher Abdullah, a turbaned black man of Jewish descent. The pair work together for five years in New York City.

1938: Neville begins his own teaching and speaking.

1939: Neville's first book, *At Your Command,* is published.

1940–1941: Neville meets Catherine Willa Van Schumus, who is to become his second wife.

1941: Neville publishes his longer and more ambitious book, *Your Faith Is Your Fortune.*

1942: Neville marries Catherine, who later that year gives birth to their daughter Victoria. Also that year, Neville publishes *Freedom for All: A Practical Application of the Bible.*

1942–1943: From November to March, Neville serves in the military before returning home to Greenwich Village in New York City. In 1943, Neville is profiled in *The New Yorker.*

1944: Neville publishes *Feeling Is the Secret.*

1945: Neville publishes *Prayer: The Art of Believing.*

1946: Neville meets mystical philosopher Israel Regardie in New York, who profiles him in his book *The Romance of Metaphysics.* Neville also publishes his pamphlet *The Search.*

1948: Neville delivers his classic "Five Lessons" lectures in Los Angeles, which many students find the clearest and most compelling summation of his methodology. It appears posthumously as a book.

1949: Neville publishes *Out of This World: Thinking Fourth Dimensionally*.

1952: Neville publishes *The Power of Awareness*.

1954: Neville publishes *Awakened Imagination*.

1955: Neville hosts radio and television shows in Los Angeles.

1956: Neville publishes *Seedtime and Harvest: A Mystical View of the Scriptures*.

1959: Neville undergoes the mystical experience of being reborn from his own skull. Other mystical experiences follow into the following year.

1960: Neville releases a spoken-word album.

1961: Neville publishes *The Law and Promise*; the final chapter, "The Promise," details the mystical experience he underwent in 1959, and others that followed.

1964: Neville publishes the pamphlet *He Breaks the Shell: A Lesson in Scripture*.

1966: Neville publishes his last full-length book, *Resurrection*, composed of four works from the 1940s and the contemporaneous closing title essay, which outlines the fullness of his mystical vision and of humanity's realization of its deific nature.

1972: Neville dies in West Hollywood at age 67 on October 1, 1972 from an "apparent heart attack" reports the *Los Angeles Times*. He is buried at the family plot in St. Michael, Barbados.

About the Authors

NEVILLE GODDARD was one of the most remarkable mystical thinkers of the past century. In more than ten books and thousands of lectures, Neville, under his solitary first name, expanded on one core principle: *the human imagination is God*. As such, he taught, everything that you experience results from your thoughts and feeling states. Born to an Anglican family in Barbados in 1905, Neville travelled to New York City at age seventeen in 1922 to study theater. Although he won roles on Broadway, in silent films, and toured internationally with a dance troupe, Neville abandoned acting in the early 1930s to dedicate himself to metaphysical studies and embark a new career as a writer and lecturer. He was a compelling presence at metaphysical churches, spiritual centers, and auditoriums until his death in West Hollywood, California, in 1972. Neville was not widely known during his lifetime, but today his books and lectures have attained new popularity. Neville's principles about the creative properties of the mind prefigured some of today's most radical quantum theorizing, and have influenced several major spiritual writers, including Carlos Castaneda and Joseph Murphy.

MITCH HOROWITZ is a PEN Award-winning historian whose books include *Occult America, One Simple Idea, The Miracle Club,* and *The Miracle Habits*. His book *Awakened Mind* is one of the first works of New Thought translated and published in Arabic. The Chinese government has censored his work.

Twitter: @MitchHorowitz

Instagram: @MitchHorowitz23